A MEXICAN RESPONSE

A Twentieth Century Fund Paper

A MEXICAN RESPONSE

BY LUIS RUBIO F. AND FRANCISCO GIL-DIAZ

Priority Press Publications / New York / 1987

The Twentieth Century Fund is a research foundation undertaking timely analyses of economic, political, and social issues. Not-for-profit and non-partisan, the Fund was founded in 1919 and endowed by Edward A. Filene.

Copyright © 1987 by the Twentieth Century Fund, Inc.
Manufactured in the United States of America.
ISBN: 0-87078-215-0

Foreword

The international debt crisis did not begin in Mexico in 1982, but the magnitude of Mexico's debt and the pronounced impact it had on the U.S. economy led the media to focus attention on the international debt crisis for the first time. Over the past five years, there has been a continuing series of negotiations between the debtor and creditor countries. Mexico has been perhaps the most prominent participant among the major debtors. Its officials have been engaged in bargaining with the U.S. Treasury and the Federal Reserve; representatives of the international financial agencies, the World Bank, and the International Monetary Fund; and a large number of commercial bankers. Each negotiation was followed by an agreement that was hailed as bringing an end to the crisis. Despite continuing austerity that brought lower living standards, Mexico's debt continued to rise, but the economy failed to resume its growth. After the great borrowing and spending spree of the 1970s, the hangover was severe.

This is the second paper in the Twentieth Century Fund series on the international debt crisis to look specifically at the problems of Mexico. The first paper, entitled *The Mexican Time Bomb,* by Norman Bailey and Richard Cohen, focused on the misinterpretation of Mexico's problems by officials of the U.S. Treasury and the international financial agencies who put together the various rescue packages intended to solve Mexico's problems, all of which persisted in treating the problem as a temporary one. Now, five years later, it is clear that that misdiagnosis can no longer be sustained.

In this second paper, Luis Rubio and Francisco Gil-Diaz take issue with some of the views expressed in *The Mexican Time Bomb.* But they agree that Mexico cannot continue to go on as it has done for the past five years. To the contrary, its authors recognize that the measures taken to deal with the debt problem have raised the threat of economic and political instability. So they argue for new steps that will build a new political consensus for the changes that must take place before economic growth can resume.

We are grateful to Luis Rubio, director general of IBAFIN, an independent think tank in Mexico City, who has written numerous articles on debt, on the politics of economic policy, and on Mexico's political system, and Francisco Gil-Diaz, professor of economics at the Instituto Tecnologico Autonomo de Mexico who has held various positions in the Mexican government, for this paper. They provide their own personal view of the current situation, not that of the institutions with which they are associated. And they suggest a way out of the current deadlock, which has featured increased debt but no growth. They believe that their proposed program can put Mexico back on the road to recovery and growth.

We hope that they are right. If they are, the debt time bomb can be defused.

M. J. Rossant, DIRECTOR
The Twentieth Century Fund
May 1987

Contents

Introduction

Foreign debt has traditionally been an instrument for augmenting limited domestic resources needed for development. All countries have, in one way or another, resorted to borrowing abroad to speed the pace of internal economic growth and satisfy social needs. With the collapse of the dollar standard and the OPEC embargo that followed in the early 1970s, developing countries adopted more relaxed fiscal and monetary policies. Like so many other countries in that period, Mexico resorted to borrowing as a means of financing its rapidly growing fiscal deficit. Debt repayment was not considered a problem since under the prevailing relaxed conditions in international markets there seemed to be no reason for doing so.

It was not the first time Mexico pursued such a course. In the early 1800s, Mexico's foreign indebtedness had direct consequences, both because of bank abuses and because of a series of defaults. But since the end of the revolution in 1917, the use of, and resort to, debt changed greatly. In the early 1940s, when public foreign debt had reached a formidable 41 percent of gross domestic product (GDP), the main trend in public management of the debt was to steadily reduce it in relative terms (as a proportion of GDP).

During the 1950s and 1960s, government policies sought to stimulate rapid economic growth and industrialization through substitution of imports without inviting accelerating inflation. On the political side, these policies were designed to increase both employment and wages. A strong political leadership and well-developed channels of participation through the Institutional Revolutionary Party (PRI), the official party, enabled the economy to attain the desired objectives—rapid economic growth with low inflation. Moreover, from 1941 through 1955, through some repayments and extremely moderate use of new debt—associated with tight fiscal policies—foreign debt was maintained basically at the same level in current dollars. In 1945, public external debt represented 16 percent of GDP, and by 1960 it constituted an even more manageable 9.5 percent of GDP (see Table 1).

Active net foreign borrowing resumed in 1955 when high levels of economic growth and small fiscal deficits allowed foreign debt to remain at a fairly constant—and moderate—proportion of GDP. Small fiscal deficits implied easily manageable current account deficits in the balance of payments. Foreign debt thus constituted a direct complement to domestic savings, which allowed prices and the exchange rate to remain stable. Consequently, relatively high and sustainable rates of growth were being achieved at a reduced cost (see Table 2).

TABLE 1
Public External Debt (millions of dollars)

Year	Debt	Debt*/GDP Ratio
1940	707	41.5
1945	671	15.8
1950	706	14.5
1955	773	10.7
1960	1,212	9.5
1965	2,183	10.2
1970	4,040	11.4
1975	12,212	13.9
1980	32,433	17.4
1981	41,786	17.5
1982	56,924	33.0
1983	60,446	42.3
1984	66,707	38.9
1985	70,553	40.0

* To obtain a long series of public external debt, balance-of-payments (BOP) flows of net borrowing were accumulated to or subtracted from a base debt (1968). This indirect method results in figures slightly different from the official ones, which are available for only a few years. The differences are less than 10 percent.

Sources: Indicadores de Moneda y Banca and *Indicadores Economicos,* Banco de Mexico.

TABLE 2
Public Sector Operational* Deficit and Current Account Operational Deficit (BOP) (as a percentage of GDP)

	Operational Deficit	*Current Account Operational Deficit (as a percentage of GDP)*
1965	0.76	2.2
1970	3.25	3.5
1975	7.53	5.4
1980	3.57	3.9
1981	11.60	5.2
1982	5.98	-3.7

* The operational concept is defined in chapter four.

Sources: Estadisticas de Finanzas Publicas, Secretaria de Hacienda y Credito Publico (SHCP), Mexico, 1981; *Indicadores Economicos,* Banco de Mexico.

In the 1970s, for both economic and political reasons, foreign debt began to grow in size and importance as a means of government financing. Indeed, the very concept of foreign debt was radically altered: until 1970, external debt had been a small part of total resources. Foreign investment from 1960 through 1970, for example, had constituted 25.3 percent of all external resources and averaged 22.4 percent of current account deficits. After 1972, foreign debt became one of the major sources of government financing, mainly the result of a rapid growth of government spending, which domestic savings were unable to finance.

Foreign resources were used not only for productive investment projects capable of repaying, over time, the swelling levels of debt. In addition, a portion was used to finance current spending and the establishment of government-owned industries that were never intended to be internationally competitive. The relaxation of international financial standards, the availability of petrodollars, and the seemingly unending willingness of international banks to channel resources made it not only possible, but even attractive for Mexico, as well as for many other countries, to hire foreign debt—and never look to the eventual costs.

The Echeverria administration increased public spending in the early 1970s because it believed that was the only way to satisfy many of its constituencies. Foreign debt was an expedient means of financing the deficit created by these increased levels of spending. The spending bonanza that foreign debt provided thus became government policy in the 1970s.

To be sure, the artificial stimulus given the domestic market through subsidies, unproductive investments, and uncompetitive new industries, and the growth of current spending through direct and indirect subsidies had a major flaw. To sustain such policies, public spending would have had to grow permanently, which would have meant a continuously growing rate of foreign indebtedness.

The question today is not whether those policies should be continued—current inflation levels and the lack of new sources of foreign debt make clear that this option is no longer available—but whether radical reforms that will allow high rates of economic growth with low levels of inflation can be carried out. After all, the extravagant policies followed from 1970 to 1982 were partly a response to the need to satisfy various critical domestic political constituencies. Today, there is an emerging recognition that change is needed in Mexico; as we see it, this new mood makes reform possible.

In this paper we attempt to explain the causes of Mexico's indebtedness as well as to assess what has to be done—and the feasibility of doing it. We begin with an analysis of the economic conditions facing the country in the 1960s and the economic reasons for relying so heavily on foreign debt. We then review the political motives for increasing this indebtedness and argue that economic circumstances and political considerations together made foreign debt an easy and expedient short-term "quick fix" for the country's problems. Then we analyze the way debt was spent and used. We go on to describe what has been done since borrowing dried up in 1982 because of what amounts to a lenders' strike, and evaluate the strengths and weaknesses of the IMF-sponsored adjustment program followed since 1982. Finally we propose a course of action for the future.

There is no doubt that the costs of the huge growth of foreign debt over the last decade far exceeded the benefits. The question now is how to confront the problems plaguing the economy and how to divide the burden of adjustment. Major adjustment is clearly called for. The critical issue is not whether but how to share its costs. Sooner or later, major foreign banks, international lending institutions, and the governments of industrial nations will have to bear part of the burden, not only by lending more, but by helping to create conditions that will promote a resumption of economic growth and bring about reductions in the relative size of Mexico's existing debt.

What must not be ignored in the search for solutions is that a program of economic restructuring, such as the one Mexico requires, also has important political implications. The domestic constituencies that would be served in adjusting to current realities are different from those that benefit from a protected economy. The crisis that Mexico has faced since 1982 has, in any event, weakened those favored constituencies (that is, some industrialists, some parts of the bureaucracy, and some labor unions), because of the failure of the economy to function effectively. In addition, a more open economy will naturally strengthen those industries that are internationally competitive and weaken the bureaucratic apparatus engaged in carrying out protectionist measures. There is ample international and historical evidence that, in the long run, an open economy is more likely to strengthen the political system than to weaken it.

Admittedly, the problems exposed by the debt crisis are complex and difficult. The experience of the last five years in Mexico, Latin America, and world financial markets has shown that the growth of debt produced a growth of problems. Yet they are problems that must be resolved. And while it would have been naive to expect major solutions back in 1982, when few had heard of the debt problem, today there is no excuse. Everyone involved is well aware of the stakes. It is time to act.

1 / Why the Recourse to Debt Took Place

After the revolutionary period (1910-17), Mexico experienced several decades of unstable economic growth. During the first part of that period, the primary task of the new regime was building a political base that would create and ensure the continuity of the political system. Though economic growth was important, it was not considered a priority, and the government paid little attention to developing economic policy. It was not until the late 1920s that the first institutions needed for economic development were established, most notably the Banco de Mexico, the Central Bank. Gradually, the government put economic policies in place, until, in the 1940s, it was effectively spurring economic growth through investments in roads, dams, ports, and so forth. Unfortunately, growth in this period all too often was accompanied by an unstable—albeit relatively low—inflationary pattern.

But from the 1950s through the early 1970s, as the result of a concerted effort, the government brought about high levels of growth with low levels of inflation. To attain stable growth, policies aimed at industrializing the country, thereby increasing the levels of employment, were pursued. But the policies pursued tended to isolate Mexico's economy from the rest of the world because they were focused on internal markets, a focus encouraged by the strong political coalition of industrialists, government, and labor unions that were at the heart of the ruling coalition. Eventually, those policies contributed to the undoing of the so-called Stabilizing Development.

The Era of Stabilizing Development

In the mid-1950s, in order to industrialize the country and create sources of employment for a rapidly growing population, the government followed the kind of steady macro policies, such as a balanced budget and investment in infrastructure, that promote price stability and, thus, allow for economic decisions that promote long-run investment commitments instead of the speculative and hedging activities so wasteful of real resources that characterize inflationary environments. These policies were particularly effective given the external economic environment, which was extremely tight and disciplined as a result of low levels of external inflation, a strong dollar, fixed exchange rates, and orthodox monetary policies.

Partly as a result of monetary price stability, which set the stage for private investment, and partly as a result of a policy of public investments that concentrated on infrastructure, the country enjoyed steady growth amidst stability. Growth was obtained with a gradually increasing (but only up to moderate and tolerable limits) ratio of public debt to GDP. This ratio was only 14.3 percent of GDP in 1965, but by 1971, it had reached 24.8 percent of GDP. Of this increase, one-tenth was accounted for by foreign debt and the rest by internal debt.

Real-interest-rate policies, which provided savers with attractive real rates of return, allowed banks and financial institutions to capture an ever-increasing share of the economy. This in turn allowed the government to increase the relative size of its domestic debt without putting undue pressure on domestic financial markets, while pursuing a reasonable claim on the country's current income from abroad to service its foreign debt. The proportion of payments on foreign public debt to income (net of government interest income from abroad) on the current account of the balance of payments averaged 6 percent in the 1960-71 period, making it easy to service the debt.

The economy had grown at a reasonable pace despite a considerable fall in the country's terms of trade, that is, Mexico's exports declined in value in the international markets compared to the cost of the goods and services the country imported. (One unit of Mexico's exports could buy 1.31 dollars of imports in 1951, but could only buy 92 cents in 1971.) Ironically, the government abandoned the Stabilizing Development policies in 1972, just before the terms of trade improved dramatically. (In 1980, one unit of exports could buy 1.38 dollars of imports, quite an improvement over the 1971 figure.)

By the early 1970s, the program of Stabilizing Development, which ran from 1954 to 1972, had given the country almost twenty years of growth above 6.8 percent per annum, while industrial production had grown an average of 9.6 percent per annum. This growth had allowed the economy to absorb most new entrants into the labor force and to increase the standard of living of the average Mexican. In fact, the very low levels of inflation allowed the population at large to develop positive expectations about the future, and these translated into increased savings, investments, and consumption.

Unfortunately, however, the policy of protecting industry against foreign imports—which had allowed for economic growth, but lower growth than would have been permitted by an open economy—had introduced all sorts of distortions. The protected markets had allowed the prices of industrial output to rise beyond the world average for the same products and, in some sectors, had promoted wage increases that surpassed increases in productivity. Then when the foremost exporting sector, agriculture, began decreasing its total exportable output after 1965, the flow of foreign exchange to finance industrial imports was reduced. The decrease in output had two causes: protectionism, which squeezed the agricultural sector through excessively high prices and low quality for its inputs, and a policy of setting prices for agricultural products that were all too often erratic and insufficient.

But what hindsight allows us to see clearly today could not be seen at the time. Furthermore, the government that came to office in 1970 and made the decisions that brought the problems to a head was faced with political considerations which, in its view, overrode other factors. The 1968 student movement described in the next chapter was a manifestation of discontent and, from the point of view of the government, dealing with that problem was critical. In addition, it had become clear that future economic growth would be limited unless significant reforms were carried out, particularly a gradual liberalization of imports and a strong commitment to exports. Instead, the government resorted to public spending in order to expand the internal market artificially. It was only the sudden advent of extremely favorable external conditions that allowed these public policy excesses to continue for years. The economy was not faltering and, hence, the coalition for growth in a protected economy remained strong enough to defeat any reform or liberalization. It was not until the last few years, when the fact that the economy had to be reformed was accepted politically that policies for restructuring the economy could be implemented. In other words, it was not until a new coalition began to emerge that reform began to be recognized, by society at large, as the only possible solution to Mexico's economic problems.

Despite having provided a stable framework for growth, not everything had been wine and roses before 1972. The good macro policies were beginning to be contaminated with pernicious micro policies as early as the start of the 1960s. This structural weakening was related to public expenditure policies; to trade and transport policy with its cobweb of rules and regulations; to the erosion in real terms of the public sector's income; and to the beginning of the government's indiscriminate involvement in the purchase and creation of firms, trust funds, and agencies across many economic sectors. Many regulations, expenditure items, and the like, were, of course, reflections of the demands and interests involved in the political coalition; those could only be altered, as in any country, when a new coalition replaced the old one.

The growing involvement of government in providing goods and services led to a politicization of economic decisions: whereas a private manufacturer seeks a profit from anything he produces, the government is always subject to pressure and criticism, and therefore makes decisions based on political considerations. Through the 1960s, the Mexican government believed that real price levels could not be maintained and/or should not be set according to the cost of providing them, particularly in the case of energy, water, sugar; some of these had been privately owned and, through price controls, fell into the public fold. The entire process required endless bureaucratic decisions, creating an enormous bureaucracy with its own interests, independent of those of the initial political coalition, further complicating matters.

Not only were large amounts of revenue being forgone, but subsidized prices meant that demands were made on the public sector to provide increased quantities of these goods and services. Thus, a substantial and growing portion of government resources was devoted to increasing electric power capacity, to purchasing and operating unprofitable sugar mills, to creating oil refineries, and so forth, reducing what was available for basic infrastructure, such as roads, railroads, seaports, health, education, and social expenditures.

Price Distortions and Public Investment

The country was engaged in a vicious cycle that was leading it into ever-higher capital requirements for investment in projects with increasingly lower returns. Public investment went from 6.3 percent of GDP in the 1960-71 period to 9 percent in the 1972-82 period, aided by the rise in terms of trade and the bountiful infusion of foreign credit throughout this period, but it was probably less productive than before.

Price controls were responsible for government involvement in areas such as sugar production and refining, which had its own bureaucracy. Market regulation brought government involvement in the purchase, wholesale distribution, and export of coffee and tobacco.

The notion that manufactured or processed goods offer protection against adverse international terms of trade, together with the legal restrictions on private-sector investment in the production of basic petrochemicals, led the government into large outlays for petrochemical plants. Production of these goods was neither timely nor economical. Some of them could have been purchased at bargain prices in world markets, and furthermore, while they are highly capital-intensive, they provide employment only to skilled workers, and Mexico had few of those. In a country where close to a million new sources of employment are needed every year to cope with a young population (over 50 percent of the population is under fifteen years of age), large capital-intensive investment projects in steel and petrochemicals at uncompetitive prices will do little to improve the welfare of its inhabitants.

This expansion in government expenditures was financed by the large volume of oil exports as well as the steep rise in the country's terms of trade. For a few years, Mexico enjoyed the benefits of a mix of exports that was highly prized in the world markets. The result was increased income—and increased availability of loans from international financial institutions for oil production. The structure of public investment thus leaned toward capital-intensive projects and, with the exception of oil exploration and extraction, meant little in the way of efficient and sustainable increased production or employment.

Trade Policy

In addition, trade policies and related programs promoting increased use of domestic goods in manufacturing encouraged private firms to produce for the domestic market only, in spite of the proximity of the large American market. This sort of industrialization led, in turn, to production on a small scale of goods whose high costs would require substantial reduction in real wages to make them internationally competitive.

Given a certain average level of protection, an increase in protection of any particular sector means that another sector is less protected—or even negatively protected. An example of the latter is agriculture. Partly as a result of having to compete at international prices while purchasing domestic inputs, such as fertilizer, seed, and tractors—sometimes shoddy products—at higher than international prices, agriculture lost ground as a source of production, exports, and employment.

The deleterious effects of protectionism presented the government with a policy dilemma at the beginning of the 1970s, as the country became less and less able to export, while requiring large imports to grow. These costs of protection were noted by economists during the Echeverria (president of Mexico for the period 1970-76) electoral campaign. But the inefficient industrial policy was "saved" by the rise in the terms of trade and by the abundance of world credit that resulted from the international oil shock. Protectionism and its unfortunate consequences, which were again called into question at the onset of the Lopez Portillo presidency

(1976-82), were given yet another lease on life because of renewed international credit and the emergence of oil exports. This time, however, the new wealth was directly controlled by the government, which over the years had become "independently wealthy."

The Macroeconomic Experience of the 1970s

Although Stabilizing Development policies had to be changed in the 1960s or early in the next decade, the 1970s did not bring the major structural reforms necessary to allow future growth. If a gradual economic liberalization process had begun, an easy transition could have taken place: obsolete industrial plants would have had access to credit to modernize; laid-off workers would have been few in relative numbers and, thus, could have been given some kind of temporary support; and so on. But the favorable external environment of the 1970s made business as usual very seductive—and the internal environment was even less favorable a breeding ground for change. After all, the partners in the coalition were benefiting, the economy was growing, and jobs were being created. Furthermore, during the 1970s, the government was becoming increasingly powerful as the economy was revitalized by oil revenues and foreign loans. It was not an environment in which a political alliance favoring broad restructuring of the economy could gain power.

But change came: the Mexican economy was hit by inflation, first as a mirror of world inflation in the early 1970s, and then as a result of the 1976 devaluation, which was caused by, at least in part, an excessive accumulation of foreign debt; the result was a balance-of-payments crisis. One of the underlying causes of the crisis was the rise in interest payments to 9 percent of the country's exports (goods and services), a figure substantially larger than the 6 percent of 1970, but still not very worrisome. The principal cause of the devaluation was the deficit on the current account of the balance of payments, that is, the difference between imports and exports of all goods and services had gone from $1.5 billion in 1973 to $3.2 billion in 1974, to $4.4 billion in 1975, and in 1976 was running at a level similar to that of 1975, before the devaluation that took the peso at one point to levels higher than 100 percent over its former level.

The large and growing current-account deficits meant that Mexicans, overall, were living beyond their means. In other words, in order to maintain existing policies and levels of growth, the country was borrowing from future spending. It was an attempt to outlive an era that had come to an end financially, but not politically.

Growth was still artificially fostered by further increasing—rather than gradually reducing—the economy's isolation from the rest of the world. This increased isolation was the result of both an autarky conception of the world and political unwillingness about introducing reform. Since reform would have been somewhat painful, there was no political backing for it; so long as autarky appeared to be cost-free, the path was obvious.

Moreover, financing the growing fiscal deficits did not prove difficult. Public sector financial requirements averaged 2.1 percent of GDP from 1965 to 1970 and, with the exception of 1970, never exceeded 3 percent of GDP. This low ratio made it possible for the authorities to maintain a fixed nominal exchange rate and, through it, to achieve price stability for fifteen years. As the deficit increased after 1972, so did the public-sector financing requirements. The deficit doubled in 1972, passing from 2.47 percent of GDP in 1971 to 4.93 percent in 1972. It kept on growing, reaching 6.86 percent in 1973, 7.25 percent in 1974, and an at-the-time astounding level of 10 percent of GDP in 1975.

To understand the enormity of these figures it is necessary to look at what was happening to the country's economy. First of all, government revenues had increased from 18.4 percent of GDP in 1971 to 23.8 percent in 1976; increased taxation had transferred resources from the public to the government. Therefore, the deterioration of public finances (that is, a growing fiscal deficit) was the result of expenditures growing at a faster rate than revenues.

The balance-of-payments crisis of 1976 led to an adjustment program agreed upon with the International Monetary Fund (IMF). The program required a substantial reduction in government borrowing, which meant reducing expenditures or increasing revenues, or both. There was a profound debate within the government as to what course should be pursued. Some argued that what was necessary was an adjustment that would, once again, balance expenditures and revenues, thus giving the private sector a major role in economic growth. Others argued that revenues could be increased and that the government should have a strong presence in the economy; hence, while a financial adjustment should take place, the thrust of the adjustment should be to correct the existing imbalance and not to restructure the economy. The only thing that allowed a deferral of action was oil; if not for oil, the coalition for no-reform, for maintaining a big, but probably not strong, government role in the economy and protection from imports, would have collapsed under the weight of economic reality—which is exactly what began to happen in 1983.

Mexico, an oil-rich nation, had begun to benefit from the price increases for oil during the second half of the 1970s, precisely at the time when the debate about adjustment was taking place. The increase in oil prices—and the promise of unending availability of foreign exchange— proved decisive, making possible the 1978-79 decision to pursue the course of high government spending. Government deficits jumped from 6.7 percent of GDP in 1977 to 7.9 percent in 1980 and to 17.6 percent in 1982. Nineteen eighty-one turned out to be a paradoxical year: on the one hand, Mexico experienced the sharpest increase in foreign public external debt—$19.1 billion; on the other hand, it was the year in which oil prices began to fall.

Then, in the years after 1982, the economy plunged from dramatically high rates of growth (of over 8 percent per year from 1979 to 1981) to negative rates of growth. The period of high rates of growth without high levels of inflation or high fiscal deficits ended as it became impossible to find anybody willing to finance the budget deficits. And, of course, it is impossible to return to the microeconomic policies of the 1960s. Internal and external conditions are completely different, and the reason for the change in economic strategy in the early 1970s was that the policies of the 1960s could not be continued without introducing fundamental reforms.

Over the years, the coalition that had supported a protected economy gradually changed. Begun in the 1950s as a coalition of the private sector (mostly industrialists), some bureaucrats, and some labor unions, through the years it allowed the economy relatively high rates of growth with low inflation and, above all, an exceptional degree of political stability. The relative balance of the three groups in the coalition gradually changed as the 1968 student movement, the discovery of oil deposits, and the availability of foreign debt made it possible for the government to become the coalition's strongest partner—and to change its terms. This led to debate about economic policy with different groups supporting very different views about the role of government in the economy. The debate was quieted by government spending on all constituencies, and it took a crisis the size of 1982 for all—or most—of them to realize that unhindered spending could not be a permanent instrument of policy. Gradually a new coalition supporting restructuring—a coalition that included the middle classes, the modern sectors of government, export-oriented industrialists, and the unions of the modern-industrial sectors—began to emerge.

From a social point of view, the 1970s was a disaster. Agriculture, which employs the largest share of the population, had an average yearly growth, in terms of value added, of only 1.6 percent in the 1971-76 period, and of 2.8 percent in the 1977-82 period. The same happened in industry, even including oil, transportation, and communications. All in all, this meant that, in spite of appearances, Mexicans were becoming poorer and that, sooner or later, the country would have to pay the costs of those years of disastrous growth policies. And that is exactly what has been happening since 1982.

2 / Politics and Foreign Debt

Economic growth and development brings important changes in the society, political system, and economy of a nation. The evolution of Mexico's economy from the 1920s resulted in social mobility and economic deprivation, rapid economic advancement and social dislocation, political demands and economic diversification.

From 1940 through 1970, Mexico's economy grew at an average rate of 6.8 percent, while its population grew at an average rate of 3.2 percent: a net gain of 3.5 percent per annum on average. This meant that the average Mexican accumulated greater wealth and higher educational levels, often moving up the social ladder. In fact, the economic boom that characterized Mexico, especially in the 1950s and 1960s, gradually changed the composition of Mexican society. The changes were spurred by the growth of industrial firms in urban settings, which shifted the rural-urban balance quite radically, bringing many Mexicans into the cities and exposing them to very different experiences. In 1940, 78.13 percent of the population lived in rural areas; in 1970, only 51.4 percent remained in those areas—and this at a time when the population grew from 19.6 million to 48.9 million (see Table 3). The shift had fundamental social and political implications. Urban areas provided higher levels of education, which changed expectations and created more complex demands upon society and on the political system; greater social mobility led to new job opportunities for women as the availability of jobs com-

TABLE 3

Rural and Urban Population

Year	Total (Millions)	Urban (Percentage)	Rural
1900	13.6	12.18	87.82
1910	15.1	13.42	86.58
1921	14.3	16.25	83.75
1930	16.5	19.77	80.23
1940	19.6	21.87	78.13
1950	25.8	28.90	71.10
1960	34.9	39.30	60.70
1970	48.9	48.60	51.40

Source: La Economia Mexicana en Cifras, Nacional Financiera Mexico, 1980.

bined with the higher educational levels they had achieved drew more women into the labor force; higher standards of living led to higher consumption patterns. Of course, not everyone benefited equally from the changes that characterized Mexico from the 1940s through the 1970s; but perhaps more important, not everyone thought they were benefiting equally.

Stabilizing Development, backed by the private sector, the government, and the unions, fulfilled the economic hopes and aspirations of Mexico's modern classes. But within the growing ranks of the middle classes, the main beneficiaries of the economic growth, there was more and more unhappiness about who was reaping the benefits of this growth. Even though it was true that those of middle-class origin could break into the political domain, frustration about the inability of some middle-class groups to participate broadly in the political system was at the heart of the discontent. The National Confederation of Popular Organizations (CNOP) and other institutions were effective mechanisms of participation, but many members of the middle classes—intellectuals, students, small business people—felt relegated to a nonparticipant role that they believed did not fit their social or economic status or their aspirations. Perceptions were probably more important than reality, and negative perceptions prevailed, clashing with the values and attitudes of a segment of the population that was rapidly acquiring not only a high standard of living but also the type of education commonly found in developed societies, where political expression is an important part of social change.

This discontent led to the organization of the so-called student movement of 1968, which was born out of the lack of attention to relatively insignificant riots that took place in that same year, and ended up attracting some sectors of the left. And although the movement never succeeded in attracting any of the unions or other traditional PRI strongholds, it was perceived as disruptive and potentially dangerous. The movement (which was similar to movements in other countries that same year) can be viewed as the result of obstinate decisions made by youngsters who were violently crushed by the government, causing major concern within the political system. Even though the latter may be the right assessment, the importance of those events was much more fundamental to Mexico's society and economy. One need only compare the extraordinary differences between the decade that preceded 1968 and the decade that followed. In other words, though the events of 1968 had a dynamic of their own, they appear to have served as a detonator for a radical break in the way Mexico had been and would be governed.

Inflation Becomes a Political Instrument

In 1970, Luis Echeverria came to office as the candidate of the official party. From the outset it was clear that the 1968 crisis had uncovered deep differences among Mexicans that the party was not prepared to deal with. The 1968 crisis was the beginning of a growing polarization among critical social and political groups. One reason for the polarization was the sharp differences of opinion about the way in which the student movement had been stopped. The other reason—cited most often by intellectuals, the private sector, students, and government officials—involved basic policy issues. Should the government be a direct participant in the productive processes, or should it be its foremost promoter? Should social justice be provided through such policies as subsidies, or should it be the result of policies that create permanent productive employment?

The Echeverria government, well aware of the issues and problems that had caused the 1968 movement, designed a government policy geared to maintain the political system by accommodating all the major political groups that had emerged during the 1968 student movement. The original intention of the Echeverria administration was reform of both the political system and the economy, but political realities did not allow for profound structural reform of the economy. Instead they led to the adoption of a policy that seemed to entail the lowest risks: rapidly growing public spending.

In his inaugural address, Echeverria made it clear that his government was not going to choose between devoting its resources to sustaining production or to social investment:

It is not true that there is an inevitable dilemma between economic growth and income distribution. Those who argue that we first have to grow and later distribute are either wrong or they lie. . . . If we consider only global figures we would say we have defeated underemployment. But if we contemplate our reality, we would have a motive for deep worries. A high proportion of our population lacks drinking water, housing, food, clothing and adequate medical services.[1]

His administration thus proceeded to pull together a coalition that would satisfy all constituencies—those who sought social justice and those who stressed the modernization of the economy; those who supported free enterprise and those who demanded rapid growth of government investments and subsidies. Rather than choosing and discriminating among various investment projects, the Echeverria government spent on all of them. The increased role of the state in the economic realm was supposed to help the government fulfill its popular commitments while diminishing social tensions; this new economic policy was to have major long-term consequences.

Under the new administration, 1971 was a year of tight fiscal and monetary policies, which set the stage for a radical change in economic policy. The following year, the program "Shared Development" was put in place; its avowed goals were rapid economic growth and income redistribution. Shared Development was used to justify the government spending spree that was interpreted as the cause of the sharp rebound of the economy by the end of 1972. But the new levels of spending led to a widening fiscal deficit and a growth of inflationary pressures. The growth of spending was much faster than the growth of revenues; hence, the fiscal deficit was overshot. And the deficit was financed by internal debt and a rapid growth of foreign debt, both of which contributed to inflation.

The public-sector spending under the new expansionist policies meant that economic growth during 1970-76 and 1976-82 was lower on average than growth during the previous twenty years. Yet, inflation, which had been kept from 3 to 5 percent during the previous two decades, rose to 12 percent in 1973 and 23.8 percent in 1974.

The fiscal gap jumped from 2.7 percent of GDP in 1970 and 0.9 percent of GDP in 1971 to 3.8 percent of GDP in 1972 and 8.5 percent of GDP in 1975 (see Table 4). The deficit, which was financed by inflation, growing borrowing from commercial banks, and foreign debt, caused a widening current account deficit in the balance of payments. The result can be summed up in the growth of foreign debt from $4.2 billion in 1970 to $19.6 billion in 1976.

TABLE 4

Public-Sector Deficit as a Percentage of GDP

1965	5.8
1966	2.9
1967	4.3
1968	2.7
1969	3.6
1970	2.7
1971	0.9
1972	3.8
1973	5.1
1974	5.5
1975	8.5
1976	7.4

Source: La Economia Mexicana en Cifras, Nacional Financiera, Mexico, 1980.

The Administration of Lopez Portillo

What Luis Echeverria started in 1970 in response to the 1968 crisis and to allay fears that Mexico's political and economic system had exhausted its reserves did not end with his administration. When Lopez Portillo took office in 1976, the political environment had become more rather than less polarized than it had been six years before. Lopez Portillo carried out an orthodox adjustment program and sponsored a major political reform that allowed formerly outlawed leftist political parties to openly participate in elections. Over the next two years, confidence and economic stability were restored, and by 1978, the economy was once again booming, with a growth rate of 8.3 percent. The discovery of major oil resources further strengthened its performance.

Almost from the outset, however, the policy disputes that had troubled the Echeverria administration reappeared. First, there were the disputes about the size of the budget cuts needed to restore the health of the economy and about oil and gas sales to the United States; then about whether to join GATT. Throughout the stormy debates, Lopez Portillo maintained his position as fence-mender. In the last two years of his administration, however, he too resorted to deficit spending as a means to maintain an unsustainable level of economic activity. For Lopez Portillo, the growth of oil revenues and the availability of foreign resources made it appear as if the country's ills could be eradicated overnight.

What made it worse for the nation this time around was that oil provided more than a new source of financing, it guaranteed a dramatic rise in foreign debt.

Until 1980, foreign debt served to finance investment projects; by 1981, however, it had become a means of replacing lost oil revenues as well as of financing soaring current spending levels. When foreign debt ceased to be a source of financing because bankers refused to roll over existing lines of credit in 1982, the economy fell into disarray, bringing a year of disaster that ended with the expropriation of the private banks and the imposition of exchange controls.

The Politics of Foreign Debt

Appeasing social tensions and political conflict is, in any country, a normal and necessary feature of government policy. That part of the Echeverria and Lopez Portillo administrations' policies was not only justifiable but respectable. What cannot be justified, particularly given the dire consequences of these policies are the means they used to try to attain those goals. The goals were never reached and the country is worse off today in levels of employment, economic growth, GDP per capita, and inflation.

According to the rhetoric of both administrations, the government's aim was to redistribute wealth and improve conditions for the poor and the unemployed. There is no doubt that, for a short while, at least, those goals were partially fulfilled (in a country of high unemployment, there was even a bottleneck of labor in 1981). But the use of inflationary financing and an excessive resort to foreign debt had enormous costs—and the success was temporary.

Pursuing even the most commendable social and political objectives in an inflationary environment provides only ephemeral gains. It makes it all too clear that the lack of structural adjustment, which should have been initiated in 1970, is the single most important hindrance to long-term recovery. That is the issue that was begged from 1970 through 1982. Foreign debt—and rapidly improving terms of trade—made it possible to avoid doing what had to be done. Now the country is paying the price of the years of public spending, both current and investment, to generate aggregate demand—thus fostering short-term economic growth—and to subsidize some sectors of the economy to alleviate political tensions. Even though spending with a political goal is, as was pointed out before, what government business is all about, spending the way Mexico did constitutes a crisis in the making.

The Mexican government's rationale for hiring foreign debt is easy to understand. In their eagerness to solve political problems, few stopped to analyze how the debt being accumulated would be serviced—and eventually paid back. Since scarcity of resources was not the issue, even those who did question the advisability of this course said little, and not too many listened. In any event, in the beginning it all seemed plausible. Most foreign lending during those years can be traced to specific projects, parastatal firms, and government programs. Some of the largest projects, like oil, were productive and profitable ventures at the time debt was hired. The situation changed only when oil prices, and Mexico's terms of trade in general, began to decline in 1981 and 1982, because of worldwide economic recession.

Explaining the rationale of the government is not too difficult, but what was the lenders' rationale? During the 1970s, the recycling of petrodollars brought enormous pools of cash into the international banking system. The underdeveloped countries, because they were starved for capital, were natural recipients of this newly created oil-wealth. Furthermore, the underdeveloped countries were attractive targets for loans from the bankers' perspective because such loans were much more profitable. Over time, many banks lowered credit standards and became "credit pushers." Of course, few in the recipient countries opposed foreign borrowing, but the banks knew they were lending far more than they should have. Growing assets, not the efficient allocation of credit, seems to have been their primary goal, which became even more evident after oil prices collapsed in mid-1981.

Until 1981, many credits were probably made to profitable ventures. After the collapse of oil prices in June 1981, however, debt increased quite drastically, often without regard to specific projects. The fact that these risks are called sovereign cannot, in all honesty, be used to deny the fact that there is a natural commercial risk in loans made to other countries and that they should be treated as such. It is on such a basis that bankers are supposed to lend. The history of bank lending during this period, however, clearly shows how bankers ignored the rules. Looking back, it is quite obvious that many loans went straight into current spending accounts. Furthermore, during 1981, bankers extended over $20 billion in new loans to Mexico, knowing full well they were not being channeled into profitable ventures. The major banks should not have been surprised when they found Mexico penniless in 1982.

The de la Madrid Years
Internally, the explosion of the crisis in 1981 surprised most of those who had advocated unlimited public spending as the solution to the country's evils. Few sectors—political, academic, or economic—had stopped to analyze what the growth of foreign debt entailed and what it meant for the future. Furthermore, nobody knew for a fact what the size of the country's total debt was until the last months of 1982. Once the country

had postponed interest payments, accounting began that finally clarified the picture. Those months marked the beginning of an often strident debate about debt management. The crisis did not create a political vacuum because of the nature of the political system (it is active in every area of social and political life) and because nobody expected it to be so massive. But it was the shocking size of the crisis that provided a major source of support for the de la Madrid administration's adjustment program of 1983.

The current government decided to adjust the economy and maintain debt servicing while improving the terms of existing debt obligations. The IMF program signed toward the end of 1982 guaranteed new bank financing for both 1983 and 1984. Hence, from the outset, the government was certain that the country's future would be threatened if it tinkered with debt payments. The latter, however, did not hinder opposition groups and parties, primarily from the intellectual left, from criticizing the government's economic program, its decision to service debt, and the austerity that followed. The left's position was essentially that the people should not be punished with austerity programs, unemployment, and declining living standards, in order to service a debt from which it did not benefit. Taking a critical stance—never recommending anything specific other than stopping debt repayment and servicing, if not repudiation—the left managed, from 1982 to 1986, to gain more and more listeners.

At the time, however, few voices advocated an outright default (negotiated or not). But by 1985, when it became clear that the country's plight was so severe that an internal adjustment would not be sufficient to restore economic growth (no matter what was done), many more people began to raise the possibility of default.

But the most dramatic shift in opinion pre-1985 and post-1985 was not on the default issue. Before 1985, most Mexicans believed that there would be some years of austerity—as in Lopez Portillo's presidency— after which growth would be restored and the crisis would end. In 1985 it became obvious that what was required was not only a financial adjustment, but a restructuring of the functioning of the key markets of the economy. Though the latter was obviously necessary, what began to emerge in 1985 was a growing recognition of the seriousness of the country's plight, of the lack of easy solutions, and of the need to make basic structural changes. What emerged may well end up being the coalition for growth in the 1990s, a coalition that would be based upon those sectors committed to export and to restructuring the economy. At this stage, however, the emerging consensus is more modest: it is consensus for change.

Further Down the Road

The political implications of these developments could be far-reaching. Not only has the old coalition been essentially buried—though many of its advocates are still preaching—but a new one might well be emerging. When, early in 1986, oil prices collapsed from $24 per barrel to below $10, a new wave of public opinion was evident. During the first few months of 1986, the government pursued a tougher line vis-a-vis the terms of the foreign debt. They argued that it was impossible to service foreign debt at current oil prices. The president's final decision was to initiate a new round of negotiations to improve the terms and payment profile of the debt.

The decision to conclude an agreement with the banks supported by the IMF and the U.S. Treasury (which was signed late in 1986) may prove to be a model for future negotiations. The conflicts over the debt negotiations of 1986, which entailed a package of over $12 billion, have made it clear to even the most orthodox government officials, opinion leaders, and others that an important ingredient in the solution of Mexico's problems is a fundamental change in the nature and conditionality of agreements between creditors and debtors.

3 / A Problem of Size and Cost

In August 1982, Mexico announced it was stopping payments on its foreign debt. Years of high and growing fiscal and external deficits, largely financed by borrowing from abroad, ended with the refusal of international bankers to roll over payments coming due. The deficit-debt cycle was finally over.

Years of high levels of growth had made it appear as if growth was a permanent feature of the economy; furthermore, the middle classes, which had often viewed themselves as among the more disaffected groups during the 1960s, lived through a bonanza period where an almost fixed exchange rate—in the context of high inflation—allowed them to travel widely through the world, buy expensive goods, and achieve a standard of living once possible only in the wealthiest of societies. Nobody should have believed that a relatively poor country such as Mexico could continue in this way for very long. After 1982, it was clear that it could not. The critical problem had become whether the debt accumulated over those years could be managed solely through internal economic reforms or whether some of the burden would have to be assumed by the international commercial banks.

How Large Is Mexico's Foreign Debt?

The size of a nation's debt is relative, depending upon the nature of its economy and, particularly, on its ability to pay. There are two ways to assess the size of a country's debt. One is to make an international comparison of debt ratios, that is, to compare what percentage of a country's exports has to be assigned to debt servicing; the other is to analyze the worth of the assets that back up the debt. Both approaches point in the same direction: Mexico's foreign debt is unbearably high.

International comparisons. The size of a country's debt has to be measured in relation to the size of its economy, its GDP, or, better, to its GDP per capita, which is a measure of both the size of the economy as well as the relative wealth of its population. In 1983, for instance, Mexico had an annual per capita income of $2,240 and a public foreign debt of $64 billion; hence, the average per capita Mexican income bore a debt of $22 million. If one compares this figure with those for other countries (see Table 5, column "Net Adjusted Debt/Income"), Mexico's debt is the highest of all the creditor countries compared, including Brazil. Furthermore, if one measures the ability of a country to service its debt by comparing interest payments with income on the current account, that is, a comparison with all exports of goods and services (see Table 5, column "Interest on Current Account"), Mexico fares just as badly. By any measurement, Mexico's debt is far too large.

The obvious conclusion is that with the halt in international voluntary lending, for Mexico to resume growth, a major change had to be made in the structure and cost of its foreign debt. Furthermore, these comparisons also show that servicing a debt the size of Mexico's is inconsistent with growth; in other words, Mexico had to choose between growing considerably less and servicing its debt. Paradoxically, a unilateral decision not to pay would not bring about higher levels of sustained growth.

Investments backing Mexico's indebtedness. A country, like a company, goes into debt in order to finance investment projects, to buy productive assets, to expand existing operations, and so forth. Analyzing the assets that "back up" a debt provides information about how likely a country (or a company) is to service its debt. Of the total public foreign debt Mexico contracted from 1971 to 1982, two large investment areas—oil and steel—went sour as conditions in world oil markets changed; for example, annual oil-related income fell by slightly over $10 billion between 1984 and 1986, a sum greater than the total interest payments on Mexico's current account for the latter year. In addition, steel exports had to be held back because of protectionist measures taken by the U.S. government.

During the 1970s, many plants were expanded and new projects were launched on the basis of the internal price of oil, which was heavily subsidized. Hence, when oil prices collapsed, these investments lost their relative advantage: now anyone can get oil at those prices. Debt associated

TABLE 5

**Public External Debt of Some Important Creditors
1983 (millions of dollars and percentages)**

Country	Average Debt	Implicit Interest Rate on Public External Debt	Adjusted*/Public External Debt	Net International Reserves
Mexico	64,259	10.6	51,214	2,096
Brazil	52,568	9.5	37,549	3,618
Indonesia	19,986	6.3	9,467	3,293
Nigeria	8,458	11.5	7,313	1,328
Turkey	15,662	7.5	8,832	-643
Argentina	19,760	10.1	15,016	983
Philippines	9,579	6.8	4,898	-10
Korea	20,755	8.4	13,108	1,494
Morocco	9,235	5.5	3,819	-297
Egypt	15,348	3.5	4,039	381
Thailand	6,619	8.0	3,981	1,078
Pakistan	9,462	3.3	2,348	995
Algeria	13,411	9.0	9,075	2,361
Portugal	9,773	8.0	6,319	1,117
Peru	7,398	5.5	3,059	889
India	20,362	2.7	4,134	3,682
Sudan	5,400	0.7	284	-342
Chile	5,981	9.3	4,182	1,381
Venezuela	12,510	13.3	12,510	7,542
Greece	7,455	10.1	5,661	990
Israel	15,024	7.4	8,359	3,654
Colombia	6,436	8.0	3,871	2,659

* Average external public debt for each country is multiplied by the ratio of that country's implicit rate of interest to Venezuela's implicit rate of interest.

TABLE 5 (continued)

Country	Adjusted Debt Net of Intl. Reserves	Net Adjusted Debt/Income	Net Adjusted Debt/GDP	Net Adjusted Debt/Income on Current Account	Interest on Current Account
Mexico	49,118	21.927	33.8	232.0	29.1
Brazil	33,931	18.048	18.1	135.0	20.2
Indonesia	6,174	11.025	7.9	29.2	4.1
Nigeria	5,985	7.772	9.3	34.2	3.5
Turkey	9,475	7.641	19.8	167.1	19.7
Argentina	14,033	6.779	19.6	177.4	15.3
Philippines	4,908	6.458	14.2	99.5	12.0
Korea	11,614	5.778	15.2	47.5	6.8
Morocco	4,116	5.416	30.9	199.6	28.8
Egypt	3,658	5.226	13.1	80.7	9.4
Thailand	2,903	3.540	7.2	45.6	6.2
Pakistan	1,353	3.469	5.2	44.0	5.2
Algeria	6,714	2.894	14.2	60.2	9.4
Portugal	5,202	2.333	25.6	113.0	16.5
Peru	2,170	2.086	12.3	72.0	12.8
India	452	1.738	0.3	4.7	1.4
Sudan	626	1.565	9.1	100.3	9.5
Chile	2,801	1.560	21.2	73.0	10.8
Venezuela	4,968	1.294	60.8	33.0	5.6
Greece	4,671	1.195	15.2	105.9	12.9
Israel	4,705	0.876	21.1	92.0	13.4
Colombia	1,212	0.847	3.4	39.3	8.8

Sources: World Development Reports, 1984 and 1985; *World Bank International Financial Statistics,* IMF-World Bank, February 1983, February 1984, and November 1985.

with investments in oil and production of its by-products has therefore also lost in value. If one analyzes the total investments carried out by Pemex (see Table 6), the government oil monopoly, one can see that during the Lopez Portillo administration (1976-82), when the big jump in oil-related borrowing took place, $28.3 billion of total debt was due to oil, not including interest.

TABLE 6

Recent Pemex Investment in Dollars[1]

Year	Pemex Investment (millions of U.S. dollars)	Implicit Rate of Interest on Public Debt	Compounded (carried forward) at 1982 Debt Values of Pemex Investments
1971	313	6.91	—
1972	307	6.71	—
1973	472	7.51	—
1974	640	8.56	—
1975	1,002	8.54	—
1976	1,376	7.71	2,356
1977	1,568	7.25	2,493
1978	2,758	8.12	4,089
1979	3,970	10.26	5,444
1980	5,500	8.07	6,840
1981	9,318	7.33	10,723
1982	5,216	7.22	5,404
TOTAL			37,349

Sources: Indicadores Economicos, Banco de Mexico, and *Fiscal Statistics,* Direccion General de Estudios Hacendarios, SHCP.

Finally, in both the 1970 and 1976 administrations, increasing steel manufacturing capacity was a government priority, which translated into the creation of SICARTSA, a huge steel mill on the Mexican west coast, whose profitability has been affected by its own internal problems as well as by the current worldwide steel glut, and Altos Hornos de Mexico (AHMSA), a steel mill located in the city of Monterrey, which was recently closed. As in the case of oil, investment in steel production was huge (see Table 7). Of the $63.3 billion of foreign public debt at the end of 1982, $41.5 billion or 66 percent are accounted for by steel- and oil-related investments.

But oil and steel are only two examples, albeit major examples, of industrial sectors for which debt was contracted that have been unable to help service those debts. Another example is the large debt incurred in the purchase of a tuna fishing fleet whose value later declined considerably because of the great fall in the international price of tuna and the embargo on Mexican tuna by the U.S. government. These examples, which are not meant to deny that there is inefficiency in many parastatal companies, add an important additional perspective to the problem of debt.

Foreign debt was also used to support the subsidies on some public goods and services (see Table 8). Although many goods and services began to be sold below cost in the 1960s, inflation—which took off in the early 1970s—induced a rapid erosion of even those prices in real terms, despite more or less frequent increases in their prices to consumers because price increases were always lower than inflation. Taking

TABLE 7

Steel Investments

Year	SICARTSA plus AHMSA Investments (millions of Current U.S. dollars)	Compounded (carried forward) at 1982 Values of Steel Investments
1971	30	69
1972	30	65
1973	56	121
1974	249	502
1975	637	1,184
1976	276	472
1977	104	165
1978	98	145
1979	92	126
1980	251	312
1981	473	544
1982	467	484
TOTAL		4,189

Source: Fiscal Statistics, Direccion General de Estudios Hacendarios, SHCP.

TABLE 8

Investments for Supplying the Increased Quantities
Demanded of Subsidized Public-Sector Goods

Year	Amount in Current U.S. Dollars	Compounded (carried forward) at 1982 Values of Former Column
1977	1,461	2,323
1978	1,353	2,006
1979	3,032	4,158
1980	5,075	6,311
1981	5,787	6,660
1982	6,318	6,546
TOTAL		28,004

into consideration only the investment required to provide the artificially expanded levels of consumption of domestic energy (including gasoline) and Mexico City's drinking water, the value of the investment had risen to $28 billion.[1] Thus, up to one-third of total foreign indebtedness could be accounted for by huge capital-investment projects to provide additional quantities of public-sector goods and services. Non-oil subsidies account for $11.9 billion of the public debt outstanding at the end of 1982, as can be seen in Table 9.[2]

TABLE 9

Subsidy-Related Investments at 1982 Present Values
Net of Oil-Related Subsidy

Year	Induced Investment Amounts
1977	1,805
1978	1,072
1979	1,718
1980	2,118
1981	2,926
1982	2,251
TOTAL	11,890

The Costs of Repayment: Mexico's Transfer of Resources Abroad

The public assumes that a debtor—be it a person, a business, or a country—has to pay both interest on its debt as well as amortization on its principal and that these are two different things. What they do not realize is that when they make their monthly interest payments, they are already paying part of the total value of the loan.[3] This is so because, even with no inflation, the value of the money being lent today is much higher compared to what it will be on the date on which the principal is due (say twenty years). This is what is called present value. A way to illustrate this point would be to ask a banker if he would accept the payment of interest on a loan for a hundred years if he would never get back the principal; he probably would not quibble very much about accepting this proposition because the principal becomes a smaller and smaller part of the original present value of a loan as the time of payment is pushed into the future.

This argument is a useful way of showing why Mexico has in fact been transferring resources back to the banks. After only five years of servicing a debt at a 10 percent rate of interest, 38 percent of the original value of the loan has already been paid.[4] (See Table 10 for material that allows this argument.) What is more, in twenty years, the lion's share of the debt is paid off, even if no principal payments are made.

TABLE 10

Proportion Paid of the Interest Value of a Loan in Which Only Interest Is Paid*

Proportion Paid	Time
9.1	1 year
38.0	5 years
61.4	10 years
85.1	20 years
99.1	50 years

* At a 10 percent rate of interest.

Over the last few years, developing-country loans have been decreasing in relative importance in international bank portfolios. Actually, the relatively large debts of 1982—which could have then imperiled the international financial system's stability—have become a manageable problem from a worldwide perspective, even though no principal payments have been made or, at most, only small nominal increases in total debt have taken place. As a result, what was impossible in 1982, namely, to reduce the nominal size of developing-country debt, may become feasible in the late 1980s.

For Mexico, with a total foreign debt (public and private) of $95 billion in 1983 and, conceivably, lower at the end of 1987, if taken net of international reserves, all of this means the country has had to transfer real resources to the banks. In other words, in spite of whatever inefficiencies and even inadequate uses of funds might have taken place from 1970 to 1982, the fact of the matter is that most assets backing that debt have decreased in value and that a real transfer of resources has taken place. Hence, not only has Mexico's strained financial system had to cope with domestic credit demands, but it has also had to finance the repayment of the country's foreign debt.

An adjustment had to take place in 1982 because there were basic disequilibriums that had to be corrected. However, the full repayment of the foreign debt is an excessive burden. In this context, no matter what adjustment is carried out—and much has already taken place in public finance and the balance of payments—an adequate rate of economic growth may prove to be impossible as long as the debt service remains at current levels.

*　　*　　*

The 1986 negotiations between Mexico and the international creditor banks are the best example of why traditional agreements and negotiations are incapable of solving the foreign exchange requirements of countries that are denied further access to international voluntary lending.

From the beginning of the negotiations it was clear that Mexico needed a transfusion of foreign exchange to tide it over the plunge in its oil revenues that had been caused by Saudi Arabia's increased oil production. But the negotiations were so difficult and protracted that, by the time the funds became available, Mexico had already adjusted to the shock through changes in its internal policies, with obvious negative results in terms of inflation and output.

It has become increasingly evident that neither shocks nor the resumption of investment at the level needed for continued growth can be financed while debtor countries have to transfer continuously a substantial portion of their income. International commercial banks on the other hand are understandably wary of increasing their exposure even more, especially U.S. banks, whose situation is even more difficult because of an overall weak portfolio (oil and agricultural loans), a lack of adequate past provisions to enable them to face the current crisis, and regulatory encumbrances. To make bad things worse, the amount of loans outstanding to several countries with difficulties makes a traditional write-off solution extremely unlikely.

In summary, the future is likely to bring a continual refusal to grant substantial write-offs, a reduced exposure of international commercial banks vis-a-vis developing-country borrowers, a resumption of growth in borrowing countries, and an extremely painful and ultimately unfruitful continuation of the prevailing mechanism for negotiations. Some conditionality and international supervision of commitments should be thrown in as well.

The powerful and contradictory forces at work may result in frustrated borrowers who are increasingly pushed into agreeing to unilateral solutions. These may be beneficial to some debtors in the short run, but will in the long run impose enormous costs across the board. What then is the solution? If banks were to lend a fraction of the interest due on former loans each year, that would be a guarantee that the part of their portfolio representing loans to troubled countries would be smaller each year, since the liabilities of banks tend to grow on the average at a rate at least equal to the rates on borrowing.[5] The debtor countries, on the other hand, would agree not to ask for additional finance until they had achieved a mutually agreed upon reduction in the relative size of their loans.[6]

4 / Coping with the 1982 Crisis

In 1982, Mexico found itself facing its worst crisis in recent history. The rapid accumulation of foreign debt had increased the cost of servicing that debt until there was no possibility it could be serviced; in addition, the reluctance of the government to devalue the peso in previous years had a number of adverse effects, among them capital flight, an enormous growth of imports, and the virtual elimination of manufactured exports. By the end of 1981, these issues were converging; all it took to detonate the debt bomb was the refusal of the international banks to once again roll over the lines of short-term credit in August 1982. Then everything went wrong: employment in the manufacturing industry fell by 7 percent; interest rates became negative by more than 65 percent; prices soared (inflation was 28 percent in 1981 and by the end of 1982 was 100 percent); and the economy shrunk by one-half of 1 percent. In September, the private banks were expropriated and exchange controls introduced. And finally, the old coalition based upon protectionism crumbled.

On December 1, 1982, the current administration came into office and immediately set out to overcome the crisis. Now, four years later, the country appears to be once again facing new difficulties, such as high inflation and a worsening performance in terms of its balance of payments. The situation is not, however, the same. The current difficulties are not the result of persistent populist policies, but of extremely harsh conditions in the external environment. It is always easy for governments to blame external forces—they are the favorite scapegoats for domestic failures—and most governments do so even when external circumstances are good and improving. But even though it is possible always to claim that more of this or more of that should have been done, the Mexican economy has been absorbing a persistent decline in its terms of trade since 1982, which turned into a dramatic fall in oil prices early in 1986.

Government Action Since 1982

The aftershocks of the 1982 crisis were severe and prolonged, as a result primarily of decisions made in 1982. The disequilibrium in the public-sector deficit was at a historic high, and that, together with the rapid debt accumulation of previous years, threw the economy into a tailspin when foreign credits were suspended. But the new government also had to cope with a loss of confidence created by the abrupt and unexpected expropriation of the Mexican-owned private commercial banks, by the establishment of controls on all foreign currency transactions, and by the forced liquidation of dollar-denominated deposits in Mexican banks.

Since Mexico's proximity and links with the United States makes the operation of currency controls unworkable,* establishing such controls caused great psychological damage: after all, over the years the population had been repeatedly assured of open currency markets. The new government thus had to cope with, in addition to a stunned population uneasy about the future, the suspension of foreign credits, considerable arrears on private-sector debt, and declining terms of trade.

The administration took over in the midst of falling production and employment and rising inflation. Its reaction was to impose fiscal discipline in order to strengthen the battered economy. The budget was trimmed through steep increases in taxes and higher prices for goods and services provided by the government, and by lowering expenditures. As 1983 advanced, wages and profits fell while the public deficit was halved, and the balance of payments showed a remarkable improvement. For the first time in over four decades, Mexico attained a surplus in its current account; that is, exports of goods and services were higher than all imports, including payments of interest on debt. Although annual inflation reached a historic high of 117 percent in April 1983, it began an almost continuous drop afterward, and at the end of the year output began to recuperate.

The recovery program initiated at the end of 1982, which proved to be an immense success, was brought about through budgetary austeri-

---

* Without going into the administrative minutiae, suffice it to say that more than five million Mexicans live in close proximity to the Mexican-U.S. border and that Mexicans and Americans cross the border about 275 million times per year, making exchange controls impossible.

ty. But the lack of foreign credit and foreign claims on the Mexican economy would have brought about an adjustment in the economy anyway. The only difference the austere budget made was a lower inflation and less disruptions in the productive processes. And there were major improvements in economic aggregates. But three things happened that prevented a complete turnaround in Mexico's financial situation. First, the financial adjustment program was not followed by a complete program of structural change. Such a program was implemented belatedly because the country entered 1983 with negative net international reserves and a highly unstable foreign exchange market that had taken the peso/dollar ratio six times above its initial 1982 level. The government believed that international reserves had to recover before the economy could be opened, a process that began slowly in 1984, and gathered tremendous speed in the middle of 1985. Second, from 1981 on, oil prices continued to fall—from almost $40 per barrel to $25 per barrel in 1985. In February 1986, oil prices collapsed to below $10 per barrel. Since oil accounted for up to 68 percent of the country's exports in 1985 and for over 40 percent of government revenue, the impact of the decline has been massive; it has made a mockery of the efforts made to reduce the government deficit. Finally, the public deficits the country incurred through the 1970s are now being paid. Thus although there has been an impressive adjustment in public finances, earlier deficits, the decline in revenue from oil, and the rise in nominal interest rates combined to produce an intractable gap in the government's accounts.

Government Finances

The main thrust of government economic policy since 1982 has been to reduce the gap between government income and expenditures. And indeed that deficit was reduced from 18 percent of GDP in 1982 to 9 percent in 1983, but has since remained stagnant at around 9 percent. From that point of view, the effort appears to have fallen short of both the avowed goals of the government and of the needs of the economy. The financial sector, for instance, has had to finance that deficit, an effort that has consumed most available resources; thus, credit for private firms for other purposes has been scarce. But the truth behind the government's figures is clouded by an "inflationary veil."

To understand the way inflation clouds the interpretation of government finances, consider the following numerical example. If someone makes a deposit of 100 pesos (or dollars) at a bank for one year at an interest rate of 5 percent, at the end of the year the account is worth 105 pesos—the original 100 pesos deposited plus 5 pesos interest. That is obvious to all. However, if we add inflation to the equation, the figures change: if, for instance, inflation is 2 percent, then 2 out of the 5 pesos of interest compensate for the loss of value of the 100 pesos deposited; the nominal interest rate should therefore be 7 percent* and not 5 percent. In this example, 100 pesos a year ago would buy exactly the same as 102 pesos today. When inflation is as low as 2 percent per year, the problem is small. However, if inflation is high, it changes the picture. If inflation is 100 percent and the annual interest rate is 110 percent, by the end of the year a bank depositor will receive 210 pesos, of which only 10 pesos are interest, while the remaining 200 are equivalent in real value to the original 100 pesos. If one spends more than 10 pesos of the 210 received at the end of the year, the original value of the deposit will be lower in real terms.

A similar thing happens to government finances.** If the government figures are separated by isolating the real rate of interest that the government pays on its debts in pesos, the fiscal deficit changes quite significantly. Since a large part (over one-third) of what the Mexican government spends goes to service its own debts in pesos, by separating the real rate of interest from the nominal one it is possible to account for the amount the government spends in paying salaries, making investments, and so forth, and how much it spends on servicing debts incurred in the previous decade which a high inflation rate has led to nominally high levels. What all this means is that the government has indeed been able to reduce its "operational" deficit quite dramatically from 1982 through 1985, to the point where it almost balanced in 1983 and 1984 (see Table 11).

The operational deficit is an important advancement in the assessment of government finance in inflationary times, but can be criticized on the grounds that inflation is, in itself, a tax that the government charges the population. This the government does through the erosion of the value of money that inflation itself produces. Hence, if the latter and other effects are taken into account, the result, the adjusted operational deficit (AOD), is a better measurement of what has really happened in Mexico over the last few years.***

In 1986, the AOD was approximately 4.6 percent of GDP because of the decline of revenue due to the fall in oil prices. If one realizes that the decline of oil revenue amounts to 6 percent of GDP and that the AOD was 3.4 percent of GDP in 1985, the obvious conclusion is that despite the huge oil loss, the deterioration of public finances was only 1.2 percent of GDP. Because of inflation, the financial deficit—the

---

* Approximately.

** The government pays interest on its own debt, say 110 percent a year; if inflation is 100 percent, then the real rate of interest is 5 percent.

*** See technical note in the Appendix, pages 67ff.

TABLE 11

Mexico's Public Sector as a Percentage of GDP

Year	Conventional Measure	Operational Deficit
1980	8.50	4.22
1981	13.45	8.82
1982	17.18	5.17
1983	12.12	1.89
1984	9.72	0.61
1985	10.54	1.08
1986	16.16	1.53

Source: Informe Anual, Banco de Mexico, 1986.

more conventional measure of the deficit, the one that includes all interest payments—overshot to around 16 percent of GDP in 1986.

The conclusion that there was an adjustment in public finances is considerably strengthened when the inflationary veil is eliminated from the figures. This has been done essentially by increasing public-sector income from 27.8 percent of GDP in 1981 to 32.2 percent in 1985, which includes direct taxes as well as sales of goods and services by parastatal firms. On the other hand, public expenditures had gone up from 41.4 percent of GDP in 1981 to 46.3 percent in 1982 and have come down to 40.6 percent in 1985. If one takes out the nominal interest payments on government debt, the figures are significantly smaller (see Table 12).

TABLE 12

Noninterest Public Expenditures as a Percentage of GDP

1981	36.2
1982	37.7
1983	30.2
1984	29.2
1985	28.5

Source: Fiscal information from the Treasury Department.

Table 12 implies that noninterest expenditures have been reduced by an astounding 9.1 percentage points of GDP from 1982 to 1985, a reduction without parallel in any other country in the world. This has been the result of lower real wages, of diminished public investment, and of some trimming of the public sector. Because real wages and investment have been depressed so much, any future budgetary adjustments will have to lean more on the reduction of the parastatal sector. Obviously, for the economy to be able to grow again, government investment in infrastructure has to be stepped up, and eventually real wages have to increase, but neither can be done at this time given the current size of the public debt, both foreign and domestic. Moreover, this austerity is likely to continue for some time to come.

If these raw percentages do not convey a solid enough picture of the budgetary performance of the past few years, consider the following examples on the income side: From December 1981 to July 1986 the consumer price index has risen 13.8 times. On the other hand, from December 1981 to August 1986 the price of bread has risen 24 times, the price of tortillas 17.4 times, the price of sugar 9.4 times, monthly telephone bills 20 times, gasoline 21 times, diesel fuel 43 times, kerosene 92 times, laminated steel 15 times. These substantial relative price increases have strengthened public finances directly, have reduced the need for transfers, and have curtailed the public investments that were necessary because of subsidized prices. Needless to say, these price increases have dramatically altered the spending patterns of the average Mexican: while minimum wages have lost about 40 percent in terms of purchasing power since 1981, prices of basic staples have increased above inflation. Many of these prices had remained stagnant for more than a decade—the subway, for instance, had charged one peso a ride from mid-1960 until 1985—so the impact of these increases may not be that harsh. Yet, the whole weight of the necessary correction has taken place in a small time frame.

Other Government Actions (1982-86)

The government has also begun to put in place other policies for dealing with its economic problems, including a gradual opening of the economy to foreign trade.

Since the 1960s, foreign trade has been managed through import quotas (controlled by import permits). These quotas have been used either to ban imports or to direct industrial production. Though the original purpose of this policy had been to permit the development of a domestic industrial base, over the years excessive protection led to inefficiency, inflexibility in adapting to internal or external shocks, and incapacity to generate exports.

The current administration started out with a tight trade policy because of the lack of international reserves. As the reserve situation improved, restrictions on imports were gradually lifted, and by the end of 1986, over 80 percent of products will have no import-permit requirements. Furthermore, in 1986 Mexico joined GATT. Though much remains to be done in terms of import taxes, the path is set for an almost complete change of policy as regards trade in the next two years.

But there is still quite a way to go in terms of industrial and trade policy. Much remains to be done about government-owned firms, but there is no question that policy has firmly changed for the first time in twenty-six years and that the gains from these changes have not been marginal. Furthermore, the recent liberalization of trade contains the basic ingredient to make it successful: it has been consistent. Even with the collapse of oil revenues in 1986, this policy has been sustained, thus providing a substantial increase in non-oil exports which would not have happened had the government clamped down with controls, as it did in previous foreign-exchange crises (1975-76 and 1981-82).

The record shows a considerable improvement in overall economic aggregates. The fact that Mexico is once again in a recession in 1986 is the result of the fall of revenue due to the decline in oil prices rather than to a major alteration of the correction program. Yet problems remain that constitute a formidable challenge to renewed growth; some are undoubtedly internal, but others lie beyond Mexico's borders.

If Mexico's enormous debt were entirely related to high-yield investments in infrastructure, education, and health, it would have enhanced the future output of the country; in other words, if all that debt had been channeled to productive projects which would have, directly or indirectly, contributed to higher levels of production, more efficiency, and more competitiveness, then that debt would not only have been fully payable, but Mexicans might be thriving. Mexicans recognize—as most bankers do privately—that the debt Mexico incurred over the last decade is far too large and is not supported by an equivalent level of assets. An obvious result is the fact that for a time Mexicans, burdened by debt, implicitly sought to evade payment through migration, capital flight, and avoidance of the established financial system as a means of saving and obtaining credit. Obviously, this behavior makes a negative contribution to the country as a whole, engenders negative expectations, and contributes to a loss of confidence.

Rather than declining in absolute numbers, total foreign debt has increased from $85 billion in 1982 to an expected $110 billion in 1987. This means the country has to pay more interest every year for money it never enjoyed, since most of the additions to the $85 billion were made to keep interest payments current. This is clearly only a partial solution, and no one should be surprised that secondary markets are discounting Mexico's debt quite heavily.

The financial adjustment has been thorough, and some people associate it with heavy social consequences. During the last four years, real minimum wages have declined by up to 40 percent and the per capita income of the Mexican people has declined by almost 10 percent. Though relatively few people have lost their jobs, few youngsters coming into the labor force have been able to get a job. At first, this does not sound terrible. The problem, however, is that expectations about the future are not precisely bright. It is a mistake, however, to conclude that adjustment measures have contributed to the downgrade in the standard of living. Despite popular misconceptions, the fact is that the foreign exchange crisis and the fall in terms of trade would have brought about a reduction in living standards which would have been even steeper, had not an orderly adjustment been implemented. On the other hand, there is no question that the crisis has contributed to lower expectations and that this constitutes a political problem.

It is possible to argue that a vicious circle of this nature can be severed if there is a rapid and large internal adjustment that changes expectations. In theory, there is much to be said for a drastic approach, particularly if it could reverse the negative expectations. However, the size of the adjustment needed, given the enormous size of the foreign debt each Mexican carries on his or her shoulders, is too large to be borne internally. Mexico's current debt problem is not too different from the reparations imposed upon Germany after World War I. Germany suffered a substantial real transfer of resources to the rest of the world; eventually, such a burden became too harsh to bear. Mexico's debt should be viewed in this light; and viewed in this way, it becomes clear that Mexico's debt burden should be shared.

The Vicissitudes of Debt Negotiations

The current perception of Mexico in the world financial and foreign policy communities is as exaggerated and unrealistic as earlier views. Back in 1978, when the Lopez Portillo administration abandoned the IMF agreement of 1976, not only did the banks focus on Mexico and begin a lending spree, but the whole world turned toward Mexico as an example of a country with a bright future. Then when the economy collapsed in 1982, Mexico was portrayed as the ugliest, most corrupt nation. A few months later, in mid-1983, Mexico was once again the top performer. The failure to adjust sufficiently in 1985 was interpreted by the world community as a new downturn. And so on.

Many of these swings have coincided with critical negotiations between Mexico and the IMF, the World Bank, and the central banks of some of the industrialized countries. Naturally, negotiations have been marred by these false pictures. The economy (and the country) have not necessarily been as bad as perceived at various moments, nor as extraordinary as portrayed at other times. Yet, negotiations—and the willingness of the international institutions, as well as the commercial banks, to actively participate in them—have depended upon these perceptions. It is impossible to blame a bank (or many banks) for refusing to participate in a given loan package if it so decides; but then those banks cannot relinquish their responsibility for having made those loans in the first place. Those banks and the world community can, however, be blamed for failing to recognize the real turning points.

Since mid-1985, the Mexican economy and political system have undergone one of the most dramatic transformations in history. Yet few foreign observers have noticed these developments. During 1986, when Mexico alone was absorbing the shock of the fall in oil prices, most observers were busy criticizing Mexico for not doing anything about its economy, while praising Brazil for its unbelievable performance. What was really happening, we now know, was that Mexico was rapidly liberalizing its economy and adjusting its budget. By now we know the outcome of Brazil's program. Perceptions can be wildly different from reality.

There is no question that Mexico has only begun restructuring its economy and that much more needs to be done. But restructuring is supported by an emerging political coalition that, with debt-service relief, might bring about a turnaround. What the future holds is unknown, but the stronger the coalition becomes over the next few years, the more profound the restructuring.

These changes are the most plausible consequences of the last five years of more or less continuous austerity, recession, and crisis. What may emerge from them is a mature society, one that can lead the way to a prosperous future. But for that to happen, the world financial and foreign policy communities have to recognize what has been done, what the nature of the plight is, and above all, that a persistence in the current size and structure of debt service cannot but lead to a poorer Mexico. And a poorer Mexico serves nobody's interests.

5 / Conclusion

The economic and political reasons behind Mexico's foreign debt are clear. So is the way that debt was absorbed by an economic structure that was uncompetitive by world standards because of its highly protected manufacturing sector; its inefficient, expensive, unprofitable, and far too large parastatal sector; and its excessively regulated environment that has hindered economic development. If noninflationary growth is to resume, the focus must be on how Mexico can deal with the domestic realities—the need to adjust the economy and the probable negative results of such an adjustment—and on how the international financial community can assist Mexico to put an end to the crisis that it helped create.

One solution might be a commitment on the part of Mexico to undertake a radical shift in the size and structure of its economy in return for a radical shift in the size and structure of the country's debt. Such a solution will require cooperation on the part of Mexico's creditors. Moreover, since such a structural change will create dislocations and political pressures, it will have to be implemented gradually. But more important, for such a program to be successful, Mexico's entire society must make a full and voluntary commitment to accept the consequences of the actions taken.

Mexicans have already withstood five years of negative per capita growth, which means declining living standards, impoverishment, and, above all, acceptance of the fact that there is little likelihood of improvement in the near future. That this has not created instability does not mean the Mexican people have not been affected by it. Rather, it reveals the almost Spartan tolerance of the people—and the strength of Mexico's unique political system. Mexico is now in its sixth continuous year of austerity and negative per capita growth, yet its political system remains strong, an indication that it is capable of bringing about the kind of restructuring the economy requires. Because it not only has maintained stability, but has done so effectively and dynamically in a period of no economic growth, there can be little doubt it can do so even more successfully once it starts growing again. In addition, the system is being rapidly strengthened by the coalition for change that appears to be emerging. Clearly, the time has come for Mexico's creditors to join in making their contribution to the country's efforts to solve its problems.

No Panacea

The costs of the adjustment will engender strong opposition among some groups. But that cannot be helped. Adjustment and structural change are unavoidable if the economy is to recover its ability to grow, providing employment for the growing population and reducing social tensions and political pressures. What must be done is to promote the kind of change that will give Mexico a competitive economic base. It will require putting in place—gradually—a bold program of deregulation. The program will have to be such that while some sectors are adjusting, new ones are being created, thus alleviating the social and political impact of the process.

At the same time that the economy is beginning its structural adjustment, something will have to be done about insufficient investment levels (domestic and foreign) and the suffocating levels of debt servicing. Solving the first problem will help eliminate the second. To the extent that Mexico designs a program of recovery that its population can identify with, debt can be taken care of through a number of mechanisms, ranging from strictly financial engineering equations through capitalization schemes and grace periods to final write-offs. And this is where the banks must play a role, accepting their share of responsibility for Mexico's excessive debt.

Entering the World Market

The world economy is changing rapidly, and the gap between developed and most developing countries is growing by quantum leaps. The only way for Mexico to service its debt and improve the welfare of its people lies in its integration into the world marketplace as quickly as possible. The availability of oil—or, more specifically, the presence of high world oil prices—combined with cash from foreign loans during the 1970s and early 1980s allowed Mexico to isolate itself from world trends, making it appear as if prosperity would never end and that no internal structural changes were required.

But today the world economy is a global economy where all goods and services, whether raw materials or manufactured goods or components, are being traded as commodities. A commodity, by definition, must compete on the basis of price as well as quality—or "high-quality/low-cost" products by world standards in the market. The most successful countries over the coming decades will be those that are less reliant on traditional commodity exports and increasingly reliant on value-added goods and services exports which are competitive by world terms. Mexico must therefore make this transition—and over a relatively short period.

Where To and Why?

A conceptual definition of what has to be done and in what direction Mexico should focus its future economic growth is not too difficult to formulate. The problem, of course, is the transition process, which, either gradual or radical, inevitably entails undermining vested interests, causing relatively important changes in employment patterns, closing plants (not necessarily in perfect timing with the opening of new ones), altering the geographical locations of new job markets, and so on. A transition period of this nature can obviously be softened by any number of mechanisms, government sponsored or, as often happens, individually generated (such as temporary family support). But whatever is done to help, some dislocation is going to be unavoidable.

It is obviously easier to talk about dislocation than to face its social and political consequences. During the transition period, a population that, overall, has experienced a dramatic loss of purchasing power, particularly by minimum-wage earners, will have to face further austerity, compounded by bankruptcies of firms. But an internally well-planned process, together with a keen eye on international trends, can enable Mexico to swiftly adjust its economy while avoiding the most troublesome social and political consequences.

The issue is not whether or not to go ahead with the structural adjustment process because of the dislocations it might bring about. It has become clear that the alternatives are unacceptable. After all, the economy has been in a recession since 1981 and not adjusting means more recession which is likely to bring about increasing chaos, economically and politically.

During the present administration (since 1982), a strong effort was made to carry out financial as well as structural adjustment. Yet, it took three years for society to recognize the depth of the adjustment necessary, three years during which Mexicans did not perceive a clear "light at the end of the tunnel." In retrospect, it becomes obvious that an adjustment could only have taken place once a consensus for change had taken shape; and that consensus has only now—and only gradually and painfully—begun to emerge as more and more people realize that without change there can be no economic growth. That acknowledgment is now obvious to all—in government, the private sector, the left, labor, and so on.

Dislocation cannot be the decisive factor in deciding whether and how to pursue the adustment program. What must be considered is whether Mexico can afford not to carry out a full program of structural change. Such a program presents obvious dangers to the country's social and political stability. But the arguments that it should not be carried out because of the danger of instability are all too often irresponsible and fallacious. Without political stability, economic development lacks content and makes no sense. The question is what policies are necessary to attain political stability and economic development. What is the use of increasing the levels of employment to impressive levels like those the country experienced in 1980 and 1981, if all those gains were lost the minute the crisis exploded in 1982 (and have worsened since)? What turns out to be socially and politically wasteful is the impact of high levels of economic growth (with the natural increase in expectations that growth brings about) suddenly followed by an economic depression that corrodes the social fabric and threatens political instability. The only way to guarantee long-term political stability is structural change now.

Unfortunately, structural change is often falsely identified with a denationalization of the economy, because it entails import liberalization and the growth of exports, and it may also include a greater openness to foreign investment. A liberalized economy undoubtedly depends more on world markets than upon bureaucratic goodwill. From that point of view, liberalization constitutes somewhat of an internationalized—as opposed to denationalized—economy. But what is most often neglected is that a liberalized economy leads to a stronger political system. That is so because, counter to general belief, a liberalized economy requires a concerted effort by society at large to open up potential markets abroad and to pursue the national interest effectively. Even more, a strong and growing economy is at the heart of a thriving political system. And so, at this stage of Mexico's development, because of its economic size and because of the size of the population, the only way to help the economy become strong—and to ensure economic growth—is liberalization.

Blueprint for a Transition

Mexico must take four steps to resume economic growth:

1. *Modernization of the legal framework governing the economy.* This would mean eliminating obsolete and counterproductive regulations; establishing a formal schedule for the elimination of import permits and a greater uniformity of import tariffs to a point where Mexican industry is forced to become efficient and competitive; allowing bankruptcies to take place; and encouraging foreign investment projects geared to the international markets, where domestically manufactured components can play a significant role. In a word, the economy should be reoriented toward world markets in such a way that the transition is not impeded or slowed down so much that the ultimate goal and purpose are lost. Politically, such a program would cancel the benefits enjoyed by the now-defunct coalition for protectionism and lead the way on the strength of the new "coalition for change."

2. *Changes in government financial policy.* There must be growth of government spending on infrastructure as well as a reduction of government current spending through subsidies to consumers and business and through the maintenance of offices and entities whose purpose and activities conflict with the development of a highly efficient economy. Tax policy needs to discourage borrowing and encourage productive investments. Public spending needs to be oriented toward making new investment possible (through ports, roads, electricity, telephones, etc.). Parastatal firms have to become as competitive as all others: There is no justification for protecting most of these firms; they should be subject to internal and foreign competition.

The best way to accomplish the goal of making these parastatal firms competitive is not only by privatizing some of them, but by introducing changes that would make them more competitive at home and abroad. One approach is to change the incentives offered managers of these firms. This could be done by announcing that all subsidies and transfers to these entities would end in a given period, say one year; managers would have that time to design schemes to turn their firms competitive; to capitalize their plants; to look for partnerships; or to close down. Most parastatal firms should be able to adjust, and the benefits would be enormous because among others it would mean a reduction of the government's deficit.

3. *Changes in external conditions.* Mexico's creditors and the governments of the industrial nations must be encouraged to play a role in the process of change. Once a credible, well-founded program of ad-

justment and structural change is in place, the banks will have a reasonable basis to reconsider their objections to alternative ways of managing the existing debt, since the program would be the best guaranty that their money is secure. It would be like a corporate restructuring, where the bank extends grace periods, capitalizes debt, writes off parts of the loan, and so on. In the case of a country with a debt the size of Mexico's, there is a need for straightforward write-offs and interest rate reductions on a good part of the remaining debt. Without such write-offs and reductions, no scheme is likely to work. The governments of the industrialized nations would have the twofold task of: a) cajoling the banks into accepting the program; and b) creating the conditions necessary for the program through specific actions in the areas of regulations, trade, immigration, bilateral disputes, and so on.

4. *Establishment of an agreement among the major social, economic, labor, political, and intellectual groups about the need to undertake basic reforms.* The consensus emanating from this understanding would be the essence of the new approach to the development of the country. Mexico already has an emerging consensus for change. The task now is to turn it into a broad-based coalition that would become the natural stakeholder of the kind of program we propose.

The coalition that appears in the process of development was born before most sectors of society came to accept, over the last agonizing five years, that profound change is necessary for the economy to recover its ability to grow. The potential coalition, which includes the middle classes, the modern sectors of government, export-oriented private-sector firms, and unions in the most promising industrial sectors, is composed of groups who, for different reasons, are opposed to the old protectionist policies and are in a position to take hold and benefit from a change to an outward-looking economy. As a result, gradually, these groups have developed a strong stake in a change in policy. Though the potential coalition is still a minority, its demands for change are often supported by intellectuals from both left and right. If successful, such a coalition could become the basis for a revival of the country's economy and for the strengthening of its political system.

What It Will Take to Implement the Blueprint

The people. For the adjustment to be successful, there has to be almost universal agreement that the results will be worth the costs. Some basic facts of life, such as the inevitability of confronting some bankruptcies and plant closures, will have to be accepted as the unavoidable cost of the process. (There are ways, of course, of softening the effect of such events.) But if recent history is of any use, Mexicans can exhibit an inordinate amount of tolerance and patience in the face of crises. Given how well Mexicans have reacted as expectations of a better tomorrow have gradually vanished, what could be expected when undergoing a transition process that little by little shows signs of better times to come?

The outside world. The IMF would have to accept major changes in the way it has traditionally assessed the performance of an economy. When an economy requires an almost total overhaul, the exclusive assessment of major aggregates may not be a useful approach. In the reform transition, an economy may experience temporary increases in the monthly rate of inflation, or it may face the need for major changes in resource allocation—such as from current spending toward investment in infrastructure, which might bring about a sudden overshooting of the fiscal deficit. Overlaps in spending may naturally take place, because a government may not be able to reduce its current spending as fast as it has to increase its investment spending. To the extent that the transition is completed within a reasonable time frame, such events should not be treated as they would be in an orthodox standby progam. The agreement reached by Mexico with the IMF in 1986 fulfills some of these requirements.

The banks would have to accept that a change in current debt service trends is unavoidable. Part of the debt will continue to be serviced in accordance with the country's ability to pay. (One ought not to forget that many a bank would be grateful, after having made loans to the then—and now—unprofitable, financially nonviable entities, to recover any part of the money they lent.) The rest of the debt would have to be partially written off, capitalized, turned into new ventures, and restructured through longer terms, grace periods, and other concessions.[1] Secondary markets have shown how this can be done, so the road is quite clear; what is missing to date is commitment.

A strong commitment by Mexico's government to launch a credible adjustment program would have to be matched by a commitment to support the program's goals through specific policy decisions and actions on the part of the governments of the other industrialized nations—especially by the United States. Those governments would have to accept: a) regulatory changes in debt-management rules that would enable banks to comply with their part of the proposed deal; b) actions on trade policy such as temporary unilateral trade preferences, but especially the elimination of trade barriers for critical export products—particularly raw materials, agricultural products, steel, textiles, shoes, and other goods which are often the object of trade conflicts; c) changes in current immigration laws so as to expedite temporary immigration; and d) the creation of mechanisms to diffuse bilateral disputes.

A good part of the shift in economic policy that Mexico must undertake depends upon the conditions and circumstances prevailing in the rest of the world. Endless trade disputes based upon parochial considerations in industrial countries[2] are certainly not a promising path for a greater integration of Mexico's economy into the world markets. The long-term solution for the current debt situation is increased trade, whereby not only large-enough trade surpluses are attained to service that debt, but also substantially higher levels of total trade—imports and exports—are reached, ensuring that the internal economies of both debtor and creditor nations are revitalized.

The Future

The nature of Mexico's problem today is not adjustment, but the best and least costly way—economically as well as socially—of going about adjustment. In spite of what has been done since 1982, much more needs to be done. The most important advantage of going about a structural adjustment today is that most sectors of society are far more conscious of the nature of the problem and are therefore less willing to oppose a major transformation. Obviously nobody is willing to sacrifice his own particular advantage, but there is a growing realization that something has to be done. That is what a consensus for action is all about.

Although the design, conception, organization, and implementation of a structural adjustment program is and should be Mexico's responsibility, it is in the interest of all creditors that such a program be successful. Banks, foreign governments, and multilateral organizations share both the costs and the benefits of such a program and, consequently, have a vested interest in taking an active role in its completion.

Furthermore, Mexico's political system is uniquely qualified to manage such a transition. Major dislocations have taken place since the 1930s, and the political system has dealt with them masterfully. The question now is how to build on that experience in order to restructure the economy and proceed with growth and development. There are no prescriptions for this. But Mexico's history is proof of the country's cohesion and of the political system's resiliency. What will emerge from a profound restructuring is a sounder economy; and that, in turn, will bring about a political system capable of leading the country into the next century. The alternative is a vicious cycle of unending deterioration.

The short-term risks that the international financial community confronted in 1982 when the crisis first exploded have been essentially overcome. The long-term risks implicit in the continued stagnation of a country the size and importance of Mexico can be staggering. What is at stake is not the country's stability, but its interminable impoverishment. Mexico must take the initiative and face the need to transform its economy. The rest of the world must do its share.

Notes

Chapter 2

1. Inaugural Address, *Excelsior,* December 2, 1970, p. 18.

Chapter 3

1. This figure was calculated considering the interest rolled over on each year's marginal investment requirements. F. Gil-Diaz, "Debt Accumulation and Distorted Growth Through Subsidized Public Sector Prices," in E. Ahmad, N. Stern, and J. Scade, *Tax System of Mexico and Pakistan Project* (Washington, D.C.: World Bank, 1986).

2. To avoid double entry, one should subtract from the figures arrived at in the last column of Table 6 the investments associated with the supply of oil earmarked for subsidized domestic consumption, which were already considered in the figures for Pemex investments and in turn allowed us to arrive at the $37.3 billion sum. This is done in Table 9, which, thus adjusted, shows that non-oil subsidies explain $11.9 billion of the public debt outstanding at the end of 1982.

3. Total value can be understood as the present discounted value of all interest payments plus the present discounted value of the principal.

4. Ibid.

5. In more technical terms, if only a fraction of interest is relent each year, the present value of a loan calculated at a particular date will continuously decrease.

6. The measurement criteria could be a coefficient of the external debt to GDP, or of interest payments to income on the current account, or a combination of both. The fraction of interest due that would be relent could be variable. It would be a function of the country's terms of trade, as in the path-breaking Mexico-IMF agreement of 1986; of its degree of budget adjustment, taking the AOD measure, or the Primary Deficit (everything but interest income and expenditures); of its degree of trade openness; of the degree of the creditor countries' openness to exports; and of the extent to which international real interest rates depart from a benchmark.

The measurement of the different variables would be supervised by the IMF. Since it involves the relending of something always less than the full amount of interest, it would invariably work toward a relative reduction in banks' exposure. Therefore, even if complicated formulas are worked out, they can be applicable with a one-quarter or one-semester lag.

The fraction of interest automatically relent would have to vary in a range of one-half to nine-tenths of the total to provide countries with real relief. This way the banks' and the countries' opposing interests may be reconciled while eliminating the costly, time-consuming, inopportune, and ultimately inconclusive process that currently prevails.

Chapter 5

1. A strong argument and stern analysis of the IMF review standards can be found in Carlos Gerardo Langoni, *La Crisis del Desarrollo* (Mexico, Fondo de Cultura Economica, 1986).

2. When the size of a problem is small relative to the total size of an economy, such as a given sector of industry, a government should not be blamed for postponing some decisions or for assuming what would be the cost of not doing anything, given the relatively small size of the problem. Many parastatal firms in Mexico were absorbed by the government through the years, rather than being allowed to go bankrupt, because the cost of not closing them appeared to be bearable in view of the overall picture. Other governments have done the same by protecting—temporarily or de facto—some sectors of an economy: automobiles in the United States through "voluntary" export quotas, or VCRs in France through endless bureaucratic procedures. There are occasions when a responsible politician may decide that society has to bear the cost of not forcing a given sector to adjust. There are times when no amount of goodwill can help.

Appendix

TABLE A-1

Federal Government Deficit and Current Account Deficit (BOP) (as a percentage of GDP)

Year	Revenue (a)	Spending (b)	Deficit (b - a)	Current Account Deficit (as percentage of GDP)
1935	10.1	7.5	- 2.6	- 3.6*
1940	7.7	6.7	- 1.0	- 0.7
1945	7.3	5.4	- 1.9	- 0.3
1950	8.9	7.8	- 1.1	- 3.4
1955	9.3	9.5	- 0.2	- 0.1
1960	8.5	10.2	1.7	3.6
1965	8.7	10.4	1.7	2.5
1970	9.6	11.6	2.0	4.2
1975	12.3	16.5	4.2	6.4
1980	17.0	20.0	3.0	4.9
1981	15.9	22.7	6.8	8.0
1982	16.3	28.7	12.4	4.0

* This figure is the 1939 deficit.

Sources: Estadisticas de Finanzas Publicas, Secretaria de Hacienda y Credito Publico, Mexico, 1981; *Estadisticas Historicas de Balanza de Pagos,* Banco de Mexico, 1981; *Indicadores Economicos,* Banco de Mexico.

TABLE A-2

The External Debt of Mexico
(December of each year, millions of dollars)

Year	Total External Debt	Public External Debt
1970	6,048.2	4,218.8
1971	6,711.3	4,615.9
1972	7,419.5	4,788.0
1973	9,993.2	6,811.0
1974	14,231.7	9,698.5
1975	20,257.1	14,612.8
1976	26,108.3	19,815.4
1977	29,338.4	22,912.1
1978	33,416.5	26,264.3
1979	39,850.4	29,757.2
1980	51,591.9	34,335.7
1981	80,261.6	53,481.5
1982	90,831.4	61,136.7
1983	94,997.3	63,357.9
1984	94,841.7	65,378.0
1985	95,504.0	68,051.7
June 86	94,552.6	67,625.7

Source: Indicadores Economicos, Banco de Mexico.

TABLE A-3

Merchandise Terms of Trade
(in U.S. Dollars)

Year	Total 1957 = 100	Non-Oil 1970 = 100
1950	127.0	
1951	131.3	
1952	129.4	
1953	126.5	
1954	115.2	
1955	106.1	
1956	107.5	
1957	100.0	
1958	89.2	
1959	87.8	
1960	80.5	
1961	81.9	
1962	76.9	
1963	81.7	
1964	78.5	
1965	76.9	
1966	78.1	
1967	77.0	
1968	81.7	
1969	80.5	
1970	88.6	100.0
1971	91.6	102.7
1972	94.0	105.8
1973	107.2	117.7
1974	124.1	111.6
1975	117.3	99.6
1976	127.6	119.8
1977	133.7	130.8
1978	124.5	121.2
1979	132.5	120.4

Table A-3 (continued)

Merchandise Terms of Trade
(in U.S. Dollars)

Year	*Total* *1957 = 100*	*Non-Oil* *1970 = 100*
1980	138.5	108.0
1981	132.3	97.3
1982	113.7	91.5
1983	103.5	86.0
1984	101.8	85.0
1985	96.1	79.6
1986	60.1	76.2

Source: Subgerencia de Precios y Metodologias, Banco de Mexico for 1970-86; Economic Commission for Latin America for 1950-69.

TABLE A-4

Net Interest Paid Abroad by the Public Sector/
Net Income on the Current Account of the BOP
Net of Interest Income (Percentages)

1961	4.2
1962	4.9
1963	5.6
1964	5.8
1965	6.6
1966	6.8
1967	7.0
1968	7.5
1969	8.1
1970	6.1
1971	4.9
1972	5.0
1973	9.6
1974	11.8
1975	9.5
1976	9.1
1977	12.0
1978	19.1
1979	25.0
1980	23.8
1981	28.6
1982	37.5
1983	29.6
1984	33.0
1985	30.6

TABLE A-5

Public Sector Fixed Investment Share of GDP

Year	Total	Government	Other Public Sector
1960	5.2	1.4	3.8
1961	6.0	1.7	4.3
1962	5.8	1.6	4.2
1963	6.6	2.1	4.5
1964	7.1	2.2	4.9
1965	6.1	1.6	4.5
1966	7.0	1.9	5.1
1967	6.8	2.0	4.8
1968	6.8	2.0	4.8
1969	6.9	2.0	4.9
1970	6.6	1.7	4.9
1971	4.6	1.1	3.5
1972	6.1	1.8	4.3
1973	7.5	1.7	5.8
1974	7.5	2.0	5.5
1975	9.0	2.3	6.7
1976	8.2	2.0	6.2
1977	7.8	2.3	5.5
1978	9.5	2.5	7.0
1979	10.3	2.4	7.9
1980	10.9	2.9	8.0
1981	11.7	3.6	8.1
1982	10.3	3.0	7.3
1983	7.6	2.3	5.3
1984	7.1	2.6	4.5
1985	6.6	2.6	4.0

Source: For 1970-80, Secretaria de Programacion y Presutuesto, National Accounts. For other years, Secretaria de la Presidencia and Informes de Gobierno, 1980 and 1985.

TABLE A-6
A Profile of Mexican Oil

	1982	1983	1984	1985	1986*
Exports[1]	16,477.20	16,017.20	16,601.30	14,766.90	6,211.80
Crude[1]	15,622.70	14,793.20	14,967.50	13,308.80	5,511.90
Volume[2]	44.60	560.00	558.00	524.90	471.30
Price[3]	28.69	26.42	26.82	25.35	11.69

[1] Millions of dollars
[2] Millions of barrels
[3] Dollars per barrel

* January-August

Source: Petroleos Mexicanos.

TABLE A-7

Annual Average of Public External Debt Net of the International Reserves of the Central Bank (Percentages of GDP)

Year	Peso Debt	Dollar Debt	Total Debt
1965	1.9	6.8	8.7
1966	2.1	6.8	8.9
1967	2.2	7.8	10.0
1968	2.5	8.8	11.3
1969	3.0	9.1	12.1
1970	4.1	9.2	13.3
1971	5.7	8.8	14.5
1972	7.5	7.7	15.2
1973	9.9	8.3	18.2
1974	10.7	9.5	20.2
1975	12.4	12.2	24.5
1976	13.9	18.9	32.8
1977	13.2	24.6	37.8
1978	13.0	21.3	34.3
1979	13.1	18.4	31.4
1980	12.8	15.2	28.0
1981	12.8	16.1	28.9
1982	14.9	30.4	45.3
1983	18.6	41.2	59.8
1984	19.2	35.4	54.6
1985	19.3	38.2	57.5

Sources: Indicadores Economicos, Banco de Mexico, and calculations of the Direccion de Investigacion Economica.

TABLE A-8

External Debt Flows
(millions of dollars)

Period	Total	Public Sector			Private Sector		
		Total	Financial	Non-Financial	Total	Financial	Non-Financial
1983	1,992.0	2,886.0	236.1	2,649.9	- 894.0	1,415.2	- 2,309.2
1984	437.7	2,613.4	977.2	1,636.2	- 2,175.7	- 415.6	- 1,760.1
1985	- 1,216.5	954.1	962.5	- 8.4	- 2,170.6	- 939.3	- 1,231.3
1986	- 1,00.7	2,009.4	1,313.0	696.4	- 2,110.1	- 665.8	- 1,444.3
TOTAL	112.5	8,462.9	3,488.8	4,974.1	- 7,350.4	- 605.5	- 6,744.9

Source: Indicadores Economicos, Banco de Mexico.

Technical Note on
Adjusted Operational Deficit

According to the conventional measurement, the financial requirements of the public sector were almost halved in 1983 but remained at high levels in 1984 and 1985. The operational deficit (OD), however, tells a different story. The OD tripled in 1981 instead of merely increasing by 88 percent as calculated in the traditional way. Furthermore, there seems to have been an important adjustment in 1982 instead of a deterioration. By 1983, both measures show a reduction in the deficit in excess of 8 percentage points of GDP, but the OD shows a surplus, which is repeated in 1984 with only a slight deficit in 1985.

The measurement of the OD is a considerable improvement over the traditional budget measure, but it too suffers from a serious inflationary distortion. When there is inflation the government collects a tax, sometimes a hefty one, through the loss in the real value of its monetary liabilities.[1] This tax does not appear as such in the budgetary accounts; there is no entry labeled "income from inflationary tax." Rather, the inflationary tax manifests itself as a lower government expenditure, because it allows the Central Bank to charge the government a lower interest rate than what it would otherwise be. Another way of illustrating this effect is by asking what real public-interest expenditures would be if inflation were brought to zero.[2] The answer is that government interest expenditures would increase: the increase, in turn, would depend on the rate of inflation prevailing before it came under control, because the rate of inflation (and the public's reaction to it) determines the extent of the inflationary tax to be lost as a consequence of a stabilization program.

Another effect of inflation on the budget, albeit of a different type, is the reduction in the tax burden because of the lag between the time the tax is due and its payment. The effect[3] is negligible when inflation is small, but it can be rather high at rates of inflation of some 60 percent per year. It can make taxation practically disappear in real terms if annual inflation reaches four digits.

The budget deficits should therefore be corrected upward, by subtracting from it the inflation tax, and downward, by adding to it the Oliveira-Tanzi effect, to find out how it would appear under no inflation. We shall define such a calculation as the Adjusted Operational Deficit (AOD).

Table A-9 presents the most economically meaningful definition of the deficit, one that eliminates the distortions of inflation. It portrays more clearly the disequilibrium observed in 1981-82 as well as the adjustment achieved in 1983-86, when the deficit was reduced sufficiently to make it comparable to the Adjusted Operational Deficits observed (practically equal to the conventional measure at the time) in the stable 1965-71 period, when they averaged 2.22 percent of GDP. The record as measured by the deficit shows a substantial correction which, discounting the oil revenue loss, continued in 1986. It can thus be appreciated that public finances have been considerably strengthened if the inflationary veil is eliminated from the conventional accounting of the public-sector-borrowing requirements. How is this reduction in the deficit evinced in the expenditure and income figures? The AOD has decreased because the public sector has fortified its income position despite the erosion that inflation imposes on the tax base and because it has reduced its expenditures.

Total income of the public sector increased from 27.8 percent of GDP in 1981, to 32.2 percent in 1985. The peak for this coefficient was reached in 1983 when it was 34.5, but it has shifted downward mainly because of the loss in oil revenues (from 16.7 percent of GDP in 1983 to 13.9 percent in 1985). But income from government firms (excluding oil) has gone from 6.8 percent of GDP in 1981 to 8.1 percent in 1985, barely compensating for the fall in federal government revenues (mostly taxes) from 11.8 percent of GDP in 1981 to 9.4 percent in 1985.

This fall in the tax coefficient occurred despite a substantial increase in taxes decreed in 1983 and should be attributed mainly to an unindexed tax system which loses ground in inflationary times because of the Oliveira-Tanzi effect and because of the deductions of nominal interest expenditures allowed in the corporate income tax.

TABLE A-9

Adjusted Operational Deficit as Percentage Share of GDP

Year	Conventional Measure	Inflationary Amortization of Peso Debt (-)	Oliveira-Tanzi Effect (-)	Reduction in Interest Rate Subsidies (-)	Inflationary Tax (+)	AOD
1980	8.50	3.27	.29	.24	1.58	6.92
1981	13.45	3.45	.30	.53	2.49	10.96
1982	17.18	10.64	.76	.31	5.17	12.01
1983	12.12	9.73	.76	.26	7.60	4.52
1984	9.72	7.65	.56	.19	6.26	3.46
1985	10.54	8.41	.64	.26	7.13	3.40
1986	16.16	13.42	.77	.24	11.57	4.59

Source: Informe Anual, Banco de Mexico, 1986.

Public expenditures went from 41.4 percent of GDP in 1981 to 46.3 percent in 1982 and have come down to 40.6 percent in 1985. However, nominal interest expenditures cloud the analysis of the spending side of the budget, so the true expenditure effort should be examined by observing the net of interest expenditures.

Notes

1. Basically, cash-plus-reserve requirements on the demand deposits of commercial banks.

2. To answer this question it is necessary to assume something about real interest rates paid by the banking sector to the public. We shall assume here that the real interest rate in the postinflationary situation is the same as in the inflationary period. If a so-called heterodox plan is adopted, as Argentina, Brazil, and Israel have done recently, real interest rates may rise considerably as inflation is reduced, and the increase in interest expenditures would be much larger than assumed in the text.

3. Called the Oliveira-Tanzi effect for its recognition by the Argentinean economist Julio Oliveira (1967) and by Vito Tanzi (1977), currently director of the Fiscal Affairs Department at the International Monetary Fund.

Bibliography

Basanez, Miguel. *La Lucha por la Hegemonia en Mexico: 1968-1980.* Mexico: Siglo XXI, 1981.

Botifoll, Luis, et al. *The Miami Report: Recommendations on United States Policy Toward Latin America and the Caribbean.* Miami, 1983.

Camacho, Manuel. "Los Nudos Historicos del Sistema Politico Mexicano." In Meyer, L., et al., *Las Crisis en el Sistema Politico Mexicano.* Mexico: El Colegio de Mexico, 1977.

Cline, William R. *International Debt and the Stability of the World Economy.* Washington, D.C.: Institute for International Economics, 1983.

Coopers & Lybrand. *1986 Annual Report on the Worldwide Economic and Business Climate.* Washington, D.C.: Coopers & Lybrand, 1986.

Cordera, Rolando, and Tello, Carlos. *Mexico: La Disputa por la Nacion.* Mexico: Siglo XXI, 1981.

Fagen, Richard R. *Capitalism and the State in U.S.-Latin American Relations.* Stanford: Stanford University Press, 1979.

Gil-Diaz, Francisco. "Debt Accumulation and Distorted Growth Through Subsidized Public Sector Prices." In Ahmad, E., Stern, N., and Seade, J. *Tax System of Mexico and Pakistan Project.* Washington, D.C.: World Bank, 1986.

———. "Mexico's Path from Stability to Inflation." In *World Economic Growth,* ed. Arnold C. Harberger. San Francisco: Institute for Contemporary Studies, 1984.

Gonzalez Casanova, Pablo, and Aguilar Camin, Hector, eds. *Mexico, Ante la Crisis.* Mexico: Siglo XXI, 1985.

Gonzalez Pedrero, Enrique. *La Riqueza de la Pobreza.* Mexico: Joaquin Mortiz, 1979.

Grayson, George W. *The United States and Mexico: Patterns of Influence.* New York: Praeger, 1984.

Grunwald, Joseph, and Flamm, Kenneth. *The Global Factory.* Washington, D.C.: The Brookings Institution, 1985.

Hansen, Roger D. *La Politica del Desarrollo Mexicano.* Mexico: Siglo XXI, 1971.

Hewlett, Sylvia A., Kaufman, Henry, and Kenen, Peter B. *The Global Repercussions of U.S. Monetary and Fiscal Policy.* Cambridge, Mass.: Ballinger, 1984.

Hofheinz, Roy, and Calder, Kent E. *The East Asia Edge.* New York: Basic Books, 1982.

Langoni, Carlos Gerardo. *La Crisis del Desarrollo.* Mexico: FCE, 1986.

Lassard, Donald R., and Williamson, John, *Financial Intermediation Beyond the Debt Crisis.* Washington, D.C.: Institute for International Economics, 1985.

Linder, Staffan B. *The Pacific Century.* Stanford: Stanford University Press, 1986.

Luedde-Neurath, Richard. *Import Controls and Export-Oriented Development.* Boulder: Westview Press, 1986.

Means, Grady E. *Statement on Economic Conditions in Mexico Before the Senate Foreign Relations Committee.* June 19, 1986. Mimeographed.

Newell, Roberto, and Rubio, Luis, *Mexico's Dilemma: The Political Origins of Economic Crisis.* Boulder: Westview Press, 1984.

Oliveira, J. "Money, Prices and Fiscal Lags: A Note on the Dynamics of Inflation." *Banca Nazionale del Lavoro Quarterly Review,* no. 26, 1967.

Penalver, M. *Brazil: Industrial Policies and Manufactured Exports.* Washington, D.C.: World Bank, 1983.

Solis, Leopoldo. "A Monetary Will-o-the-Wisp: Pursuit of Equity through Deficit Spending." World Employment Programme Research Working Paper. Geneva: International Labour Office, 1977.

———. *La Realidad Economica Mexicana: Retrovision y Perspectivas.* Mexico: Siglo XXI, 1970.

Tanzi, Vito. "Inflation, Lags in Collection and the Real Value of Tax Revenue." International Monetary Fund Staff Papers, no. 1 (1977).

Tello, Carlos. *La Politica Economica en Mexico 1970-1976.* Mexico: Siglo XXI, 1979.

Weintraub, Sidney. *Free Trade Between Mexico and the United States?* Washington, D.C.: The Brookings Institution, 1984.

FUNDERBURG LIBRARY
MANCHESTER COLLEGE